an
AFRICA
notebook

Also by C. W. Gusewelle

A PARIS NOTEBOOK

an AFRICA notebook

by

C. W. GUSEWELLE

THE LOWELL PRESS / KANSAS CITY
1986

Cover design and chapter art by Dorothy Day
Back cover photograph by Anne Gusewelle
Photo page 21 by Jennifer Gusewelle;
pages 110, 112, 113 and 201 by
Anne Gusewelle; other photographs by the author.

Library of Congress Catalog Card Number 86-82805
ISBN 0-932845-24-X

This book was photocomposed in Janson type and
printed on acid-free paper
in the United States of America by
The Lowell Press, Kansas City, Missouri.

ACKNOWLEDGMENT

Many of the pieces in this book
originally appeared in
The Kansas City Star.

For Bob and Anita

A PERSONAL NOTE

The writer of these essays first traveled to Africa as a young man in the early 1960s, at a time when colonialism had just given way before the impulse of people everywhere to rule themselves. New nations had been born in exultation, hope, inexperience and enormous need. Anyone who saw Africa then—who knew Africans in that brief, heady moment when the future lay unmarked before them and all seemed possible— was destined to carry the memories for a lifetime. Africa becomes a lasting presence in the mind.

In the more than twenty intervening years, much has changed.

One hears little mention, these days, of Africa's once-exciting possibilities. In the appalling headlines that seem to burst every few months onto the newspaper page, one hears only of Africa's failures and disappointments. The somber question that now is asked—that thoughtful Africans ask themselves—is whether the continent ever can surmount its handicaps and claim a place of influence in the world.

The intention here has not been to present yet another "large-picture" assessment of Africa, of the sort which, overtaken by events, so quickly becomes dated and useless. Rather, the aim has been to *narrow* the focus as far as possible; to present, through the limited window of immediate experience, an intimate sense of Africans and of life in a small corner of that vast and wonderful and suffering part of the world.

Hope, illusion, helplessness, betrayal, affection . . . all the multitudes of human beings share them. But, in the end, they are experienced singly by individuals, one at a time, each in his own place and way. And in such small stories, each one standing for the many, may be the best chance of understanding Africa, if so immense and truly fabulous a place ever can be understood at all.

The second, and more selfish, reason for the project was the writer's wish to show his daughters Africa—if only a fraction of it—while they still were young, in the absolute faith that it would have the power to claim their imaginations and in some way to expand their view of life's amazing possibilities, as so many years ago it changed his.

Dakar, July 22, 1986

an AFRICA notebook

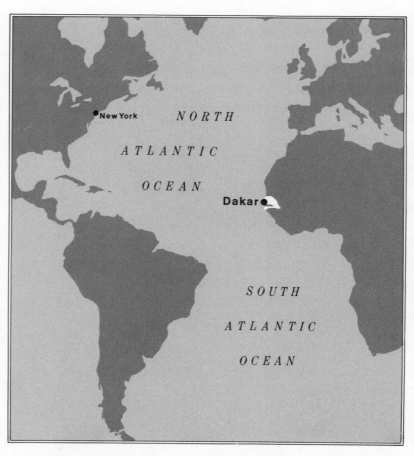

1

I N THAT DARK HOUR the coast is announced first by a slight lowering in the pitch of the engines' whine. Sleepers begin to stir themselves, rubbing eyes, feeling about for their parcels.

The plane's riders are an assortment of humanity: Frenchmen outbound to what used to be the colonies on errands of commerce or diplomacy; Japanese with contracts in their briefcases; two nuns in habit; many olive-skinned Lebanese returning to tend their shops after visits to their shattered homeland; a group of young Germans in sandals and rough clothes; at least one family of Americans. But mostly the travelers are African, and most of those are men—long-limbed, fine-boned men, elegant in dark business suits or in the cool, loose-hanging robes that are their traditional and more usual dress.

The machine tips. From its left-hand windows, out of the night, a spangle of lights is revealed. That is Dakar, the westernmost city of the continent, built on a narrow out-thrust peninsula whose shape is defined exactly by the lights and the surrounding featureless darkness of the sea.

The wheels drop and the plane shudders, slipping more steeply down the dark. Now fainter spots of illumination can be seen spaced far apart and without evident pattern out on what must be the water. Those would be lanterns carried in the slender pirogues of fishermen who are casting their nets to fill tomorrow's market stalls.

To the east, the inland side, the salting of man-contrived brilliance extends a bit—then sharply ends. There are no lighted roadways or other radiant signs of habitation that lead away from there, suggesting more bright places a little way beyond. No, the city to eastward is bounded by a darkness as final as that on the seaward side. For to the east lies the whole great body and strangeness of inner Africa, where lights are far between.

The plane touches, rolls and stops. And the riders—the gowned and the suited and the disheveled—climb burdened down a metal stair into a soup of moist and tepid air, still heat-charged with the memory of day. Fifty steps across the tarmac is the arrivals terminal, inside which all is purposeful confusion. Vaccination records must be checked and found in order. Passports are examined, questions asked, notes made.

Beyond a low barrier, perspiring greeters display hand-lettered signs, each with a name. *Mansour*, says one sign. *Reynolds*. *Deschamps*. The greeters search the addled faces of the arriving unknowns for sudden little detonations of recognition and relief. There may be nothing finer, when arriving at a late hour in so strange a place, than to see one's very own name held aloft on a piece of cardboard.

In the stifle of a crowd, suitcases are heaved off the circulating belt and onto a porter's cart. A confidential word is whispered by the porter to a uniformed customs man, who tiredly waves the cart through untouched. For this miracle the porter asks a sum which, depending on his estimate of a traveler's exhaustion and befuddlement with the strange limp currency, may be anything from a half-day's to a week's local wages. Money is exchanged. Car motors come alive on the drive outside. Singly or in groups, the travelers are borne away.

The driver, Alioune, has come in a van for the family of Americans. He is tall, quietly assured, with sympathetic eyes and a graying mustache, and he remembers the American from another year. Kind, dark face lighted by the dashboard glow, he points the van along the airport road to the city, alert to the many opportunities for calamity: Reflectorless bicycles, dusky figures in duskier clothing two paces out onto the pavement, unlighted horse carts, suicidal goats.

For several miles the sea laps close to the road, breaking on stones, frothing in the car's headbeams at the turns. Then the way mounts up past yellow-lit rectangles of humble doorways, and soon becomes a broad avenue of larger buildings.

"The office of radio and television," Alioune announces in French. "The information ministry . . . the ministry of interior." He veers off the traffic circle into a smaller street, on whose left side rears a vast, sand-colored building. "The Catholic cathedral," says Alioune. With its domed and turreted exterior washed by lights, it might more likely have seemed a mosque.

Confused, displaced in time and space, the riders are delivered past landmarks they cannot remember or later place. The van halts before a gated wall. The gate guard bounds from his chair in the shadows, and out of darkness another man appears, both of them in what seems to be some kind of uniform. Behind those two comes a figure all in white. It is the housekeeper, Khadi, who also remembers the American. She is petite and soft-mannered, with a sweet shy face, and as regal as a queen in her finest linen gown.

A key is delivered. By no conscious will of the astonished travelers, suitcases disappear inside the house and are put in upstairs rooms. With a last word of welcome, Alioune drives away into the night. The many people vanish—back into the shadows or into quarters somewhere behind. The door bolt is thrown, and the journey has ended.

There are many ways of arriving in Africa, and over the years the American has tried several of them. He has been deposited by the vagaries of travel in unexpected backwaters, not just ungreeted but unsure even of a bed. Or arrived politically unwanted and been clapped immediately into an airport lodging that was, in fact, a kind of jail. Or been cast out onto steamy, alien streets, burning and shaking with fever, speaking no language useful in that place. He decides that, decadent or not, he prefers this way of arriving.

The closed upstairs room is suffocating. But the glass doors beside the bed hinge inward. After those there are screens, and after the screens are louvered metal doors that swing open onto a balcony, letting in the verdant breath of the night.

The room cools. So much has happened that already the journey is like something distantly remembered. The dazzling plate of a full moon, seeming very large and near, shines whitely on the contorted, smooth-barked branches of an unfamiliar tree. From down below, in the darkness at the edge of the garden, floats the thin, soft mutter of the gate guard's transistor radio. The travelers are home.

2

‏T‏HE FAINT PULSE OF THE WAKING DAY beats earliest in the quick, light slap of rubber-soled sandals along the street below the window. Somewhere far off in this city of a million densely compacted souls a rooster sings, inspiring a chorus of replies. At 6 a.m. in summer, it still is midnight dark.

By half past the hour, a premonitory stain as pale as lemon tea begins spreading up the sky behind the trees. Small birds whistle and twitter their airy *matins*. Presently, the white-banded rooks strike up, coarsely complaining from somewhere in the highest branches, then flap heavily away in the direction of the sea—which, here, is nearly any direction.

By 7 o'clock the morning is fully arrived. And exactly on the hour, dependably as any worker punching the clock, the old woman comes to take her place on the sidewalk against the outer courtyard wall of the museum on the avenue's far side, the folds of her loose garment drawn close around her in the hour's brief coolness. Every morning except Sunday she sits there, a brown cloth spread before her and on it a dish for coins. There is no dishonor in her occupation. Allah looks with favor on a generous heart. So besides being her means of living, begging also is a service to those who give.

At 7:30 a short, comradely exchange of men's voices is heard below. The night guard is leaving and the senior man, Moussa, is taking the daylight watch. But first, while foot traffic along the walk is light, he steps across the street to spend several minutes speaking respectfully with the woman against the wall. He bends to put a coin in her dish. And then, that daily decency done, he recrosses to his station inside the gate.

Moussa is an old commando of many campaigns and many wounds. His bearing is soldierly and, though he is slight of stature, you sense that he has been the kind of man—a sergeant, most likely—who was solid all the way through and whom other men could depend on in any kind of scrape.

His face is wonderful, rich with wisdom and the patient good humor of someone who knows that, just as people are made in different skins, they also come in every shade of mendacity and goodness. He accepts lives as they are given.

A good part of his was spent fighting other men's wars—the Frenchmen's wars. That took him almost around the world. He speaks six languages, Chinese among them. His pension is the equivalent of $95 a month, and so in what ought to be retirement he comes to sit twelve hours a day and guard a gate. The wound in his arm, and another where a Vietnamese bullet passed through his calf without touching bone, he never notices. It is the one in his left upper leg that still pains, especially in the first chill of morning, or in late July and August, when the rains begin seriously to come.

He sits in a metal chair just inside the entrance, passing his prayer beads absently between his fingers, calling greetings through the gate to other old soldiers and friends as they go by. And when the sun climbs above the trees at the back of the garden, he moves his chair a little so that his leg can receive the

Moussa, the old campaigner

comfort of its warmth.

Next to appear after Moussa is the gardener, Dialo, in whose charge is everything green: The bougainvillaea that spills its vines and blossoms across the wall; the hibiscus and the flowering trees; the pomegranate and banana trees always fruiting beside the kitchen walk; the monster climbing philo-dendron with wrist-thick stem and umbrella leaves that has made its way almost to the upper eaves of the house. The gardener's shears can be heard *snip-snipping*. Then he starts the sprinkler turning on the walled-in square of lawn. Even in a part of the world savaged by more than a decade of drought, some uses of water are essential.

A bit past 8 o'clock the housekeeper, Khadi, comes round the corner of the porch, not begowned now but in her clothes of the working day—a day that will be shorter or longer, depending on what disorder the people in the house have made the afternoon and night before, and on the amount of laundry and pressing to be done. Khadi's home is in the south of the country—the region of Casamance—and her children are there, cared for by relatives. But her work is here. She lives with her husband in the separate small building behind the bananas and the pomegran-ates.

Finally, at half past 9, a lively step sounds on the outer walk. It is Bocar, the cook and real key figure of the household, speaking a friendly word to the others and then hurrying on to the kitchen to read the news of last night's soccer matches while he boils and filters drinking water to refill the bottles he keeps stocked in the refrigerator. After that there is lunch to make.

In the heat of afternoon, Moussa out by the gate removes his sandals and his beret. Using water from an empty one-pound Folger's coffee can, he washes first the crown of his head, then his face and arms and hands, and finally his feet. Thus suitably cleansed, he unrolls a straw mat and kneels, perhaps with pain, to perform his devotions of that hour. Afterward, for a torpid

The gardener, Dialo

Khadi in the afternoon

while between the cleaning up of one meal and the starting of the next, Bocar and the old soldier, who are friends in spite of the twenty years in age between them, sit together in the shade and quietly talk. Khadi and the gardener have finished and gone.

The light softens. Evening begins early to gather. Soon lights in the house go on. Bocar has laid the supper table, and Moussa has left the gate in the charge of the night man. Sometime in the eleventh hour after he arrived, Bocar once more puts the last of the scrubbed plates back on their shelves, runs a professional eye over his spotless kitchen and, locking the rear door after himself, hurries for the bus that will carry him to his home and children thirty more minutes away in another quarter of the town.

The gate guard's radio mutters from the darkness of the garden. A slight stir of coolness comes breathing in from the sea. Another moon hangs above the crooked trees.

For all of them, that is the invariable cadence of the days, one following the last in perfect replication. Those are the duties in houses of the city where the *toubabs* live, the pale outlanders. Such houses give employment, which is good, because the *toubab* requires much care. But the work is long and often thankless. The white man in Africa is truly the black man's burden.

3

T HE SENSE OF AFRICA as a static and essentially passive presence in the world is wrong, probably in many respects but certainly in one. The most immediately obvious of its transforming powers is its ability to change people—sometimes for better and sometimes for worse. What is sure is that if they come here and stay long enough to let Africa get its hold on them, they *will* be changed.

Maybe it is just the heat. In this season when the dry, dusty wind blows steadily out of the furnace of the desert, turning the sunsets crimson and layering the top of every leaf with a fine ocher powder, all of Africa in that wide band below the Sahara—the Sahelian zone, as it is called—waits thirstily for rain.

The smallest exertion brings a rush of perspiration. Every task is contemplated in advance, always with the furtive notion that it might be put off or, better, forgotten altogether. There is much expectant talk about when the rains will come. But some years the rains fail. And often, when they do come, the heat worsens. Yet there are parts of Africa where the days are moderate, the evenings cool, and where autumn actually brings frost. Even the desert itself can turn bitter after the beating sun has given way to the icy clarity of stars.

So heat cannot be the whole explanation.

Just as corrosive, perhaps, is the endless waiting—and not just for rain. Waiting for papers to be completed and officially stamped. Waiting for currency to be exchanged, with multiple documents painfully hand-written to legitimize each transaction. Waiting, waiting while a small repair is made. Urgently needing some item which can be gotten only in one shop that shut its doors at midday and will not reopen until half past 3 o'clock in the afternoon. Waiting to learn which official can grant a favor, among all the others who are powerless. Waiting, in an economy organized on a system of leisurely haggling, while the seller eases his price downward in grudging stages from his original ludicrous demand to something nearer the value of the goods—which may take minutes, hours or even days.

Waiting.

Yesterday, on a major avenue running alongside one of the ministries of state, three lanes of traffic came screeching to a halt and remained motionless for several minutes, the drivers to the rear honking in bafflement and impatience, while a brown-and-gray speckled hen deliberately herded her brood of six fluffball chicks from one street curb across to the next.

But bureaucracies everywhere are ponderous, and though the daily vexations may be different from place to place, life nowhere is very convenient anymore. So waiting does not, alone, account for the debilitation.

Probably the most morally satisfying explanation for why the outsider is so susceptible to being changed by Africa is the amount of pampered ease that can be had here by anyone with even a reasonable amount of money. In a place where *need* is the first thought of every day, the first law of life, money will buy for often very ordinary people a brand of care and coddling that elsewhere would be available only to the quite fabulously rich.

But if there were nothing more to it than that, then it stands to reason that all outsiders would be affected in the same degree. And obviously they are not.

Wherever they have managed to stay on in Africa, the British have their clubs and their teas and their cricket matches. Here in the western parts, the French still have a far-flung empire of bakeries to produce their croissants and *baguettes* and sweets; they hear at every hand their native tongue; they are up and out early in the morning, as they would be in Paris or Lille or any other French city, walking their peculiar looking dogs on leashes and letting them foul the footway.

Then there are the Lebanese, who are everywhere in West Africa and in great numbers, dominating middle-size to petty commerce in every town of any size. The Lebanese are a special case. They have always been a merchant people in a more or less permanent diaspora. Too industrious ever to go slack, they have followed the compass of commerce, and wherever they have found themselves, their single-minded instinct for making business has sustained and steadied them.

The point is that some people seem to need familiar trappings and familiar forms, the more so the farther they happen to wander. And Africa, in its mystery and vast differentness if not actually in miles, may be about as far away from known things as it is possible to get. Travel the continent long enough and you will see a lot of dissolute and burned-out cases. Curiously, a good many of those seem to be Americans and Scandinavians, perhaps because they have no colonial experience and have not managed to figure out which portable trappings of their culture—croissants, afternoon teas and such—they must bring along to keep themselves whole and safe.

That's one way it can go. People can weaken here, grow listless and ineffective. Or they can become stronger and more resourceful. But one way or the other they will change.

The house the American family is living in is a borrowed one. The friends whose house it is are away on leave. They were met a long time ago, more than twenty years ago, when they were young and newly married and had just come out to Africa for the first time. The American, who also was young then, was getting over a bad spell of malaria and the couple had offered an island of hospitality in a generally difficult place.

They were very idealistic. They objected on principle to having a housemaid and cook and gardener and all the other services that are generally assumed to be essential to make life bearable for the European.

This powerful place captured and kept them. Except for a few years spent in the States and a short time in Italy, they have spent most of their adult lives and reared their five children in one part or another of Africa, including the country of Zaire, the former Belgian Congo, which surely is one of its least pleasant parts.

And, yes, it has changed them. They have become somewhat resigned, understanding that realities cannot always be made to yield to high principle. They do not object anymore to having servants. In the world as it is, some people toil with the talents they are given, freeing other people to be productive in different ways. It isn't the freedom that's wrong—it's the *waste of it.*

So these friends have worked hard. Exotic transients, they have gone from one African post to the next, carrying hardly anything with them except family pictures, some pieces of authentic art and their personal library, which has grown over the years into a fabulously eclectic collection of more than 2,000 books. Whenever they arrive in some new place, that's what they bring with them in boxes and trunks and crates—along with their clear sense of purpose.

In Boswell's biography of him, the writer Samuel Johnson

quotes a Spanish proverb to the effect that, if you set out to find the riches of the Indies, you have to take the riches with you. Which is to say that any possessions of real value are inside oneself.

That's how it seems to be in Africa, where, against all the forces of ease and disintegration, it is only their character that keeps people from going soft.

4

A SENEGALESE MARKET is an example of free enterprise at work in what may be its original and purest form. No price is fixed. All is negotiable. The weekly expedition for groceries therefore becomes a kind of bloodless combat, a test of nerves and will. And while the number of eager vendors should give an advantage to the buyer, a lot—no, *everything*—depends on who is doing the bargaining.

The household is like a ship whose able seamen could bring her through any tempest and safely home if only the confused and incapable captain would stay out of the way. On marketing day, pretense goes overboard and Bocar, the cook, frankly takes the helm. He simply needs to know how many Senegalese francs, at 350 to the dollar, he's expected to spend.

There are several regular supermarkets in the city, shelves and frozen-food counters stocked with every imaginable kind of imported goods. At their cash registers, money disappears like smoke. No responsible master of the kitchen would dream of patronizing any of them, except in the deepest emergency.

Ten minutes away by foot is the Sandaga market. The

Kermel market, which Bocar prefers, is only five minutes farther. Both are traditional bazaars, centered in enormous crowded halls inside buildings of Moorish design, then spilling on outside and continuing along the street in a maze of canvas- and tin- and wood-roofed stalls. Either would be an easy walk, except for the weight of all the produce that will be coming back in the large woven basket that Bocar has gotten down from the top of the refrigerator.

So the double locks of the garage are unfastened, the outer gate opened. And with Moussa, the gate guard, waving directions and stopping traffic, Bocar looking on anxiously and various other men and boys converging to help—the *toubab* being assumed unable to get under way unaided—the borrowed car is backed into the street with a ceremony only a little less elaborate than the launching of a new aircraft carrier.

On the thoroughfare that approaches the market there is room enough for a car, with possibly two feet of clearance on either side. In those two feet, hundreds of people walk. By a miracle, a place is found to park. Small boys appear and the cook engages two of them, one to watch the car and the other to carry his basket.

Bocar's usual manner is an engaging mix of pride and lively good humor. His step has a spring when he walks. He has cooked in a hotel in France, and also in the Ivory Coast. He likes what he does and he knows he is good at it—without being in any way unbecomingly vain. He is the kind of man you like immediately, and feel glad and lucky to be around.

But now, as he approaches the vendors' stalls, a subtle change comes over him. His movements are slower, more deliberate. His expression becomes a bit less open, his habitual friendliness subdued. He has gone into his marketing mode. The produce sellers cry out happy greetings from behind their bins. They all know Bocar. He distributes his business fairly, favoring from one week to the next the stalls on different sides of the market.

Kermel market lady

Bocar, captain of the house

He lets his eyes rest indifferently on a stack of carrots. *Excellent carrots*, the woman vendor declares. *The best carrots in the whole Kermel.* As if distracted, Bocar glances languidly along the alleyway of stalls, each with its heap of incomparable carrots. His eyes move back to her stack. And what might be the price of those carrots? He holds his market list in his hand, and his money with it, the bills just visible enough to be tempting and to make clear that he is a buyer of serious intent.

Four hundred francs the kilo, the vendor says. Bocar's face registers regret, and he begins to turn away. *Three hundred francs*, she tells him. With the barest flicker of revived interest, he eyes the merchandise again. But perhaps they are not even today's carrots, he suggests sadly. *Two hundred fifty*, the woman says, putting some in the pan of her balance scale. On the other hand, Bocar tells her, if the price were 200 francs he would take two kilos and would be spared the inconvenience of having to buy carrots at one of the other stalls. He knows it is the fair price, and she knows he knows. Weighed out before his eyes, they go in the basket.

And so on down his list: Tomatoes, fresh green beans that snap noisily when bent, lettuce, the sweet little orange-meated melons, mangoes—each item bargained over with courteous determination. Not one franc is surrendered injudiciously.

He knows, for example, that eggs priced at 2,800 francs for thirty inside the main hall can be had at exactly half that from a stall outside. He handles and inspects each egg for possible damage. Then he stops at a wooden table of chickens, plucked but with their feet and feathered heads still on. The seller asks 2,500 francs for a bird that appears to have perished of hunger—its breastbone sharp as an axe blade, with no sign of meat on the sides. Bocar might pay 1,200 for it, even for one like that, but there are few chickens that day and he knows agreement will be impossible and so moves on.

At one point, a bystander in a tan robe and skullcap chimes in

23

uninvited. *Why waste time bargaining? They are Americans*, he mutters. *They have enough money. Imagine what they must spend on alcohol.* Bocar turns his eyes levelly on the man. He is buying food, he says, not alcohol, and he has but a certain number of francs to spend.

He makes a last stop for potatoes and beetroots. Except for chicken and fish, then, the week's provisions are laid in. It will be better to go in late afternoon to Soumbedioune village just up the coast road when the *pêcheurs* bring in their long pirogues, and the catch of the day—fishes of all sorts and sizes, eels, prawns and crabs—is laid out on the sand and sold directly.

The small bearer is listing severely under the weight of the basket, but seems well pleased with the coin Bocar gives him for his hour's work. Back at the house, the garaging of the car is an event as elaborate, involving nearly as many people, as the spectacle of its emergence.

Bocar, seated at the kitchen work table, is reconciling his accounts. On his shopping list he has noted the price paid for each item. It annoys him that he cannot make the change work out. Of the 10,000 francs he began with, he can account for 8,800. But, see, he has only 1,000 francs left. The shortage amounts to less than sixty American cents.

Three times he adds up the numbers. Then finally he lays out his purchases on the counter for a new inventory. His face brightens. *The tomatoes*, he exclaims in triumph. He had intended to get only one kilo, but they had been especially plump and nice so he had taken two kilos. The mystery has been solved.

Anyway, it is suggested, he shouldn't worry over so small a sum. But he shakes his head at that. About the expenditures of the household, Bocar says, one needs to be exact. It's better. He says that without any hint of rebuke, but a bit awkwardly, as though it were a thing so obvious that a professional finds it strange to have to explain.

24

5

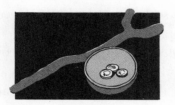

LANGUAGE IS IMPRECISE. Words serve as the symbols for ideas, but often without suggesting gradations of meaning, without beginning to convey the infinite variety of forms and degrees in which, in reality, the idea may be clothed.

Pain is such a word. Happiness is another. *Poverty* may be the most imprecise word in all the languages of man.

It is much talked about—the poverty of the Third World, a poverty abject and absolute. Yet the images the word evokes in the mind of someone of the northern latitudes, especially someone of ordinary experience, bear no more resemblance to the truth of the condition as it is experienced here than poison ivy bears to leprosy or indigestion to a cancer of the bowel.

Never mind all those Africans who work regularly and hard, who give generously of their talents and their loyalty and receive too shamefully little in return. That is the injustice of luck and historical circumstance, but it is not poverty in any real sense.

The men and boys who sweat away their years at rows of

treadle sewing machines in the half-light of streetfront tailor stalls, the women who sit from morning to night on the sidewalk and pray to catch some buyer's eye with their little heaps of nuts or bruised fruit, the piecework weavers whose fingers are raw from hours at their looms, the children who haunt the markets hoping to be asked to carry a basket or bring someone a tea—they are not poor, as Africa knows poverty.

Even the peddlers of cheap trinkets and bogus jewelry who plague tourists along the arcaded perimeter of the Place de l'Indépendance, cajoling and bullying and fastening themselves to pedestrians like some bipedal species of leech, finally become tolerable. They are opportunists, living by their wits. To the pompous and well-connected who pass by in chauffeured Mercedes-Benzes they may be invisible as ants. But they are, in their way, part of the economy. And they are not in the final sense poor. They carry in them a germ, at least, of some expectation or other.

Poverty is the nightmare that lies beyond—*incredibly far beyond*—any of that.

It is a thousand milky-eyed old men, blinded by some disease that two dollars' worth of medicine might have cured, clinging to sticks by which children lead them as one might lead a beast, stumbling and waving their empty alms bowls, through a hungry night that never breaks a dawn. And it is the children who do the leading.

It is the people simply fallen down in weakness or discouragement and bedded directly on the scalding sidewalk in the full heat of the tropical noon.

It is the legless and armless beggars who come swarming toward the car at every stoplight, pressing their faces to the window and crying their muffled pleas through the closed glass.

It is the awful, hopeful grin of the leper as he shuffles out of a doorway to display his fingerless hands. And the men and women and children of every age that one sees everywhere, heaving themselves along crablike with incredible exertions, using whatever they have left of knuckles or knees, swinging and dragging their shriveled and fantastically contorted back parts after them.

That is the constant, everyday nightmare of the street. And that is poverty. One learns when going anywhere to keep one's eyes fixed directly to the front. That is no guarantee of easy passage. It helps, though, because the worst is usually to the sides.

And it *always* is there, always somewhere close. Get caught and slowed in a crowd and it will reach out for you, insistently tapping your arm, grasping your sleeve or plucking at your trouser leg—the eternal beseechments of a poverty that no gift of a coin can touch. Poverty so bottomless that you dare not turn and look.

One day, on his way to somewhere, already bludgeoned by the heat and with the car windows rolled shut while he waited for the traffic signal to change, the American happened to glance up at the rearview mirror and was horrified at what he saw coming at him from behind down the very middle of the street. Some kind of beggars' congress, it must have been, because they all were there—the blind and the maimed, the club-handed lepers and the deformed swinging themselves on their hands. *All of them.* Those who could were waving their stumps, their mouths working and seeming to be crying out something as they closed very fast on the car.

It was as though the mirror suddenly had opened like a window directly into the howling torments of the Underworld, the worst region of it. If the light hadn't turned at that moment, it's probable he would have fainted or at least screamed.

He gave up whatever it was he'd meant to do and instead went directly back to the house. He threw the double bolts of the door and lay down on the bed in the cool room and thought about what he had seen, analyzing what he had felt—which in that moment, he had to admit, had not been so much pity as terror and a kind of fathomless revulsion, of which he was not proud.

Eventually, people who live here promise, you learn not to see all that, or at least not to be so affected by it. But the ability to get used to it is not something to be very proud of, either.

And Dakar, they say, is one of a few cities in Africa where things still go reasonably well.

6

THE AUBERGE ROUGE is an oasis of quiet civility, whose narrow doorway off the Rue Jules Ferry gives refuge from the dazzle and grinding disorder of the street. The place is run by a Frenchman. It has a dark little bar with eight wooden stools and, past that, a small courtyard restaurant. Upstairs are several rooms for lodgers.

Half the restaurant is open to the air under a scented canopy of flowering vines. To the side is a roofed area with more tables, to which patrons may retreat in case of rain. On this Sunday afternoon the American and his friend, Saliou, sit at one of the tables under the vine. The sun has passed far enough from its zenith to leave the courtyard in shade, and a cooling breeze flutters the corners of the blue-checked tablecloths.

Saliou has returned that morning from a visit to Louga in the north and has carried back a basket of ripe mangoes for a gift. They struck up an acquaintance some weeks before, while the American was transacting a bit of personal business. Since then they have met several times to drink a juice and talk at a cafe.

Saliou is from the far south of the country, from Casamance, and he is a self-made man. His marks at the *lycée*, or high school, were good. But he had no opportunity to go on to the university. So in his youth he spent a year laboriously translating a book in English, word by word, to learn the language. And after that he took a course by mail from a British university to improve his new skill.

Then he came to the capital, running errands at first and doing other small jobs. Eventually he managed to find work of a menial kind in the offices of a foreign-owned company. He applied himself, was noticed for his diligence, was gradually promoted. Until finally he achieved his present responsible position in the firm. At the age of 30, he goes each day in a business suit to his place in an air-conditioned office, where he deals directly with clients and with money—often considerable sums of money—and even has occasion sometimes to use his English, which by now is very good.

In a part of the world where advancement usually is the result either of a privileged upbringing or of family or political connections, Saliou's career has been the exception. To his less-lucky or less-motivated friends, he appears to have made a huge success and to be secure for life. But he does not feel secure. Quite the opposite, when he thinks about the future he often has an uneasiness that is close to outright fear.

He speaks of that now, as the waiter brings their salad, halved avocados filled with shrimp.

"There are two reasons why I am afraid," he says. "The first is because I have no real education in business. The things I have been given to do—my own duties—I understand very well. But only that. There still is much I do not know. In our company there was a man who received a promotion to an area of responsibility he did not truly understand. One day he had to make a decision, and he made the wrong one. It was not a mistake for his own benefit. It was an honest mistake, but it cost the company a great deal of money and he had to resign.

"And because I know nothing of theory or of business administration, only what I have learned from doing my job, I am afraid that one day such a thing could happen to me."

He toys distractedly with the food before him, and the hand that holds the fork trembles a little. His anxiety is real.

"The second fear," he continues, "is what will become of a man like me if bad times come to Senegal. *Worse* times, I mean, because already the situation is bad enough. But suppose things become worse, and companies find they must cut their staff. They will say, '*We can keep this man and this one, because they have their diplomas. And, oh yes! We must keep this man because of his family. But Saliou,*' they will say. '*Saliou has no connections, and not even a diploma. He knows only what we have taught him.*' So it will be someone like me who will have to go. If the times become worse, I think it will happen that way."

He spreads his hands in a gesture of helplessness. But just to have unburdened himself seems to have lifted his spirits.

"There is no one I can talk to about this," he says. "My friends would think I am foolish. My mother in Casamance would think I am foolish. But in fact it is a danger. That is why until now I have not taken a wife. I would like to marry, of course. But it would be unfair to a woman, who would look at my job and would have certain expectations. And who would not be able to understand that *it is supported by nothing.*"

How does he imagine the situation can be changed?

"I have a plan," he says. "I do not know if it is possible, and I would like to know what you think. But my plan is to see if there is some way that I can take a degree in business at an American university, even at my age. Perhaps there are scholarships available. And I can work. Suppose that when I finish I am 35 years old. It does not seem to me too late to begin again."

He looks at the American.

"What do you think?" he asks. "That it could be possible?"

The American in his life has known enough young Africans and their crazy, brave seekings ever to doubt that it might happen.

"Anyway," Saliou says, "I will give one year to this, to see what I can find. And then, if it turns out to be impossible, at least I will know that I have tried."

7

LIKE PLANETS FIXED in their separate and immutable orbits around the same faint star, the several worlds of Africa sometimes pass very near, often in clear view of one another. But the weak body that regulates their motion, the often barely visible sun that is The State, lacks force enough to bring them in conjunction or make them one.

The first world is the city—compacted, malodorous, energetic in a kind of desperate and inchoate way, full of incredible disparities of luxury and want, and, like most cities in the poorest nations, gradually running down as crushing debt and swollen numbers and general futility overload all its systems.

Yet it is in the city, for all the incongruities and multiplying horrors, that the slight gravitational pull of The State is most strongly felt. The clever and ambitious are drawn there by the chance of commerce. The politically adept are drawn to privilege and power. And the poor, the unskilled, the displaced from the countryside are drawn by imagined opportunities they seldom find—arriving, indeed, like migrants from a different

A thirsty ancient, the baobab

planet, only to discover a brand of hardship that is lonelier and more degrading than the communal poverty they fled.

To traverse the centuries, the light-years, between the several worlds of Africa, one doesn't need a starship. An automobile will suffice.

The paved highway from Dakar runs eastward past the town of Rufisque before making the first of its several branchings. To the north, a long half-day, is River Region and the old colonial capital, Saint-Louis. There the Senegal River empties into the Atlantic after making a sinuous arc across the top of the country, past occasional villages that hug close to the life-giving flow. Beyond the river lies another country, the wasteland called Mauritania, much of it a howling emptiness of sun-smitten desert.

If, instead of turning north from Rufisque, one takes the road on more or less straight east, one comes eventually to the frontier with the Republic of Mali, also desiccated and in places barely habitable, although it does have a government and a capital, and nomadic peoples are said to wander over much of it in those years when it happens to rain.

Some people will tell you that the trip from Dakar to Bamako, Mali, by car takes four days. Others say five or six. The truth is you rarely meet anyone who actually has attempted the journey overland, even in the dry season. The travel books are ominous in their cautions—noting the scarcity of fuel stations, advising which spare parts to take along and spelling out exactly, in liters per day, the minimum amount of drinkable water that is required to sustain human life in desert or near-desert conditions.

It is unnecessary, anyway, to mount any such expedition as that to see the second of the African worlds. For barely an hour's drive inland away from Dakar, one already has begun entering the barren and forbiddingly inhospitable Sahelian landscape.

The coastal pines and stands of mixed hardwoods give way first to isolated small plantations of coconut palms. Then even the slight luxuriance of the palms disappears, as if the relentless sun had simply burned the earth to a sterile ash.

Stretching away as far as the eye can see is the unbroken hot *levelness* whose monotony is relieved only infrequently by patches of low thorn scrub or spectral, widely spaced stands of baobabs, which Africans sometimes call "the tree that grows upside down." With its enormous trunk and its gnarled, ludicrously diminished upper parts, the baobab is a tenacious survivor, marvelously adapted to hold moisture and give almost none back into the air, dropping even its few sparse leaves as the dry season advances.

Several of those, seen together at a distance across the heat shimmer of a reddish plain, give the impression of a clan of naked, fat-bodied giants, waiting through the cooked centuries for deliverance from their hell of thirst. The ground between them has cracked open in crooked fissures a hand's breadth wide, in whose blackness no bottom can be seen.

The last thing the mind can conceive of is anything animate enduring there. But in the blinding haze something can be seen to move. As one comes nearer, the confused image resolves itself into a little flock of spavined goats. And beyond the goats is the grotesquely elongated figure of a man, scratching furrows in the dust with a stick, bending to drop seeds in the scratch, praying to whatever gods he knows that the sky will one day open and bless his hunger with a harvest.

And shortly after that there materializes a dismal hamlet—a cowering huddle of mud-walled and grass-roofed huts, intermixed with more durable shanties of boards and sheet tin. Beside the highway squats a line of women whose "market" consists of one careful stack after another of perfectly identical fruits. There may be a gasoline station, or maybe not. Always there is one tiny store, hardly more than a stall, on whose shelves a sad jumble of small tinned and packaged things can be glimpsed in passing.

As quickly as these few observations are registered, the hamlet is behind. Then there is only the road again, drawing away to a line and finally to a point somewhere ahead in that cracked and fevered landscape.

That is the world of this part of Africa, inland from the city and the sea. To see it is to grasp the reality of lives spent utterly without options. For surely, given any choice in the matter, no one would deliberately abide in so maliciously hostile a place.

This is what one might see if one continued eastward for day after repetitive day. Or, instead, one can take the road that branches south after Rufisque, passing down what the Senegalese (or perhaps it was the French) call their *Petit Côte*, the Little Coast. That road leads to yet another African world—the one that luck and money and a little water can make.

8

ONLY TWO HOURS BY CAR out of the capital, but seeming very far from the city's desperate striving and farther still from the life-defeating thirst of the all-but-unpeopled Sahelian country-side, lies this other, this most incongruous, of Africa's worlds.

It is a world built on sand and water and money—foreign money—and it exists mainly to give pleasure to the pale *toubabs* who come down from Europe to take the African sun without, if possible, letting Africa's realities intrude on their amuse-ments.

And the beaches *are* spectacular. Southward they reach in a gentle seventy-mile curve almost to the delta of the Saloum River, one following the other like pearls of rare perfection all assembled on a single strand.

The white sand is soft and fine as flour. The Atlantic, warmed here by the sun and hospitable currents, washes in invitingly over a gently sloping bottom whose smoothness is interrupted only by tumbling shells and shell fragments. Strong tides and undertow make some Senegalese beaches treacherous for swimming. But these beaches of the Little Coast are safe as any pool. Backed by a narrow fringe of coastal forest, brushed by steady and refreshing breezes from the sea, they simply curve on for mile upon mile, each one bending out finally to a distant headland beyond which, unseen, is another just as fine.

From December through the northern winter, the Europeans come in numbers to escape their native cold. They arrive on excursion flights, are met at the airport by vans or climatized buses and are borne around Dakar and directly on south to Poponguine or Somone or another of the beach places. The French know this stretch of shoreline well. So do the Germans, and perhaps a few others. But the Little Coast of Senegal is a well-kept secret from most of the other pleasure-seekers of this world. And therefore its real season is short.

Yesterday, in the hotels fronting on the water near the village of Sali-Portudal, there was a little rush of weekend people down on an outing from Dakar.

Pale men wearing the paunch of prosperity, and their equally pale and prosperous-looking wives—who should be forbidden by international law to bathe topless on a beach in Africa or *anywhere*—sprawled on cushioned mats under grass-thatched umbrellas, ordering drinks and dainties brought down to them from the hotel restaurant. A resident Frenchman looked on indulgently as his children entertained themselves by digging out and murdering the inoffensive little sand crabs, so delicate and translucent that they seem almost to be made of glass. The best word in any language for the quality of spitefulness, *méchant*, is the one used by the French.

Another man occupied himself for two futile hours by trying to stand up on a wind-surfboard, climbing onto the thing, tugging at the sail, capsizing, then doggedly climbing on again—endlessly, joylessly failing. Until finally he stumbled panting from the water and flung himself on a beach mat alongside his male companion.

That was yesterday. Today the place has all but emptied out. The hotel's three terrace restaurants have their tables all prettily

Portuguese man-of-war, Petit Côte

set, but no one comes for luncheon. Along a mile or more of white sand beach and sparkling sea only eight figures can be seen. One of those is the same man back at his grim contest with the wind-surfboard, while his friend, in a yellow bikini, oils his body and waits impatiently under a thatch. Another is an African woman of the hotel staff, passing along the beach walk with an incredible burden of jars and plastic buckets balanced in a large pan on her head.

The resorts here all were built with European and perhaps some Middle Eastern capital, and though they provide a little local employment, most of whatever they earn is exported to fatten pockets elsewhere. So this opulent other world of Africa remains, for the present, separate and sharply defined. Its blessings do not spread far.

Within the grounds of the hotel, sprinklers turn over emerald lawns that never know a drought. Small striped lizards sun on the tiled walkways. Fat monitor lizards hunt in the garden, and birds as brilliant as living jewels dart among the lush and ever-manicured flowering foliage. Exactly at the edge of the grounds, another ecozone begins—cinder-dry and relentlessly depressing.

Just beyond the garden, screened by a hedge of trees, a gray horse whose every bone is visible stands dumbly starving in a field of dust. Under no circumstance may he trespass across to eat and live. The only creatures, in fact, that pass with perfect freedom between the world inside the hedge and the world outside are the mosquitoes.

The same mosquitoes bite the tourists as bite the Africans in the village farther down the beach, where the only vocation, apart from fishing, seems to be making poor necklaces and other gewgaws out of shells the nets happen to bring up. For the *toubabs*, who take their weekly chloroquine tablets and keep safe, the bites are an itch and an annoyance. In the village, malaria is a fact of life, and death.

41

9

ALL THROUGH THE STIFLE of middle afternoon, between the cleaning up of lunch and the time for starting supper, they can be heard talking out by the side of the house nearest the gate, the cook and the old gate guard, Moussa.

A bower of vines shades them. The dry wind as it comes cornering around the house gives a slight impression of coolness. The voices of the two friends are soft and languorous, their slow conversation interrupted by quiet laughter and by long, satisfied pauses—the voices of men who know that, amid the vexations and uncertainties of every day, this time is entirely and inviolably theirs.

The cook Bocar's affection for the old man, and his concern for him, are touching. Today, after putting the noon dishes back in their cupboard, the cook spoke of what was worrying him. He didn't actually raise the subject. It came in answer to a question. Evidently he knew the people well enough, now, to believe they would understand.

Were things all right with Moussa? they had asked. *The old man seemed troubled, somehow. Or maybe it was only the worsening heat.*

"He is tired," Bocar said. "Old and tired. And Moussa is *malade*. He is sick. There, and there, and there—." The cook touched himself in the places where, during campaigns in Algeria and Madagascar and Indochina, the old soldier had suffered wounds. "Every day he has pain. But principally," Bocar said, "Moussa is tired."

The hours on the chair beside the gate, while the sun wheels in its livid arc across the garden, must be interminable—lonely hours, except for the one or two spent talking with the cook. Moussa always crosses in the morning to give a coin to the woman at the museum wall. Sometimes African children come and he speaks to them through the wire of the gate, his face serious but his eyes alight and his voice teasing. They are devoted to him.

Always toward the end of afternoon an elderly French woman passes along the sidewalk with a little boy of three or four, who must be her grandchild. They stop outside the gate, and the child waits for his flower. Moussa goes to pick one blossom from the garden and, bringing it back, presents it like the most wonderful of gifts, which to the little boy it seems to be. He and the old French woman also are in some way Moussa's friends.

Whenever it pleases someone to go in or out, he opens the gate and shuts it again behind. At the appointed hours, he cleanses himself with water, unrolls his mat and stiffly kneels to pray. Eventually the sun becomes less fierce, the shadows longer. Somehow it gets to be evening. The night man arrives, and Moussa, his duty finished, goes to catch his bus.

Those are his days.

But times are hard now, Bocar said today—hard not just for the old gate guard but for all the small Africans. He didn't say it in a complaining way, but just to state a fact. A loaf of bread that used to cost the equivalent of twelve cents has gone up to nearly forty cents. That's how it has happened with most things in recent years, a threefold increase in prices. Bread has become too expensive for many Africans to eat, although in Bocar's own house, by being careful with money, they still manage to take bread once a day, at breakfast.

But Moussa, he said, has special problems. He has more than one wife and many children. Some of the children are grown, but several still are small. The grown ones have no work. Also, his wives have brothers, and the brothers, too, are without jobs—at least one of them with no job for ten years. The trouble, Bocar said, is not Moussa's salary, which is a good salary by African standards and is, in fact, greater than his own. The problem is that whole extended family of idle dependents, all looking to Moussa for their sole support.

"He gives his money each month, and there is nothing left for himself," Bocar said. "Before, when things were not so hard, he was able to eat bread in the mornings. And he used to take a coffee, which he enjoyed very much. But now that is impossible. Sometimes, in the evenings, he buys candy to take home for the smallest children. But never anything for himself. He leaves his house at 6 o'clock in the morning, or even before 6, and he is not home again until after 8 o'clock at night. And in all that time he is without any food, because if he takes food then he will have no money for the bus.

"A man his age," Bocar said, "should have a small shop, make business, sell some little things. But he does not read. Moussa speaks many languages, but he cannot read or write or do numbers. So it is no good, a shop. And now he is *très, très fatigué*—very, very tired. But he cannot stop working, or they are all fallen."

The cook spoke the word *fallen* with a tone of finality. To fall, in a place like this, is to fall off the edge of the world.

The people sat at the table, their coffee cold in the cups before them, looking at the cook with slack, astonished faces. The old gate guard was so dear, so unfailingly friendly. They never would have suspected anything so awful.

What can be done? they wanted to know. For surely there was some way to make things right. Or at least better.

Bocar only shrugged. "It is complicated," he said. "And for many Africans it is the same now. Very hard."

Looking down afterward from an upstairs window, they saw the old man get up from his prayer mat, brush off the knees of his trousers and put on his beret, pulling it down over his white rim of hair. His face was like a face carved with great skill and tenderness from a piece of polished black wood. Then they saw the cook come out the door and around the corner of the house, and heard the two voices come up, soft and companionable, from the shade of the vine through the suffocation of the slow afternoon.

10

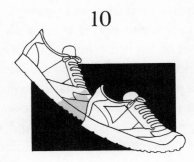

SMALLPOX HAS BEEN ELIMINATED as a scourge of mankind. At last report, there was not a single case of it anywhere in the world. But poliomyelitis still takes a regrettable toll in places where the vaccine does not reach. And the list of other dangers in Africa is long: Schistosomiasis, malaria, typhoid, leprosy, meningitis, cholera, AIDS, sleeping sickness, river blindness, the yellow and dengue fevers, and perhaps others to which scientists have not yet put a name.

What Africa obviously does *not* need, then, is a new disease imported from the West. Yet one has gotten a foothold here on the coast, has very quickly taken on the proportions of an epidemic and, for all anyone can say, might sweep out of control across the continent.

A great many of the younger men of Dakar appear to have been seized by a rage for physical fitness, that tragic ailment that manifests itself in incessant and uncontrollable *jogging*.

In Western societies—in the United States, for example—the disease's origins are plain enough to see. Rich diets, obesity, occluded arteries, muscles gone to jelly from too much ease and all the other symptoms of a generally unhealthy lifestyle drove folks panting into the streets for vanity's sake, and to save their lives. But to see the phenomenon repeated here is both sad and a little funny.

The Senegalese, taken all in all, are an uncommonly hand-some people, long-limbed and slender, with hardly an ounce of fat anywhere. What's more, once they have survived the hazards of infancy that afflict any poor society, they must have one of the healthiest lifestyles on earth. The observant Muslims among them—and followers of Islam are more than four-fifths of the population—take no alcohol. The use of tobacco, though on the rise, is nowhere near as prevalent as in Europe or the United States.

The diet, at least here in the city, consists of rice, vegetables, local fruits, an occasional stringy chicken in the pot, but principally the delicious fish that are found in such variety and abundance in the coastal waters. A fat Senegalese might fairly be called a rarity. Too much of the wrong kinds of food is practically unheard of in this part of Africa. The more common problem is too little food of any kind, but no one has ever recommended running several miles through the African summer as a remedy for hunger.

The Senegalese do not go soft behind desks in air conditioned offices. Or very few of them do. Physical activity is an inescapable part of life. Automobiles, although present in great numbers, are for most Africans an unattainable luxury, so travel by foot—even over considerable distances, but certainly for routine errands of the day—still is the usual way of getting around.

People here are passionate for sports, especially *le football*. At almost every hour of daylight, on any scrap of open field, men and boys of all ages can be found surging back and forth in adept and furiously good-natured games of soccer, often with no equipment except the ball and two large stones placed to mark the goal mouth. So for the healthy, those lucky enough not to be crippled or enervated by some real affliction, a reasonable degree of fitness is almost an inevitable way of life.

Yet the disease of the West has come here.

So joggers drive their lean and already superbly conditioned bodies along the streets morning, noon and night, daring cars and buses to hit them—not a challenge you want to issue lightly here. And they look as bored and as unhappy doing it as runners do everywhere.

Recently, a formal exercise area was set up on a tract of high, stony ground along the corniche, overlooking the sea that washes in and breaks on the rocks far below. A regular running course was laid out, with barriers to be hurdled and climbed over, bars for doing pull-ups and other little torments along the way. The number of people it attracts on any given day is astounding—hundreds, perhaps thousands. And they, too, all look unhappy as they perform this faddish but, for them, perfectly superfluous Western ritual under the full hammering glare of the sun at a latitude more than eight degrees south of the Tropic of Cancer.

Apart from the continent's indigenous ailments, history tells that many of the diseases that earlier ravaged Africans were carried in on the ships of the outsiders who came bearing glass beads, gin, Adidas T-shirts and other cheap trade goods. This new plague Africa just might not survive.

11

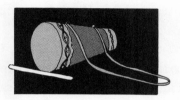

IT IS SOMEWHERE TO GO when the sounds and smells and astonishments of the city have begun to seem routine; when the sense of Africa as it has become threatens to overpower the other resonances of the place: The unfathomable strangeness upon whose ashes all the new things rose, the bizarre and inscrutable faiths and fears by which, in certain of its inner parts of forest and scalding sand, Africa still is ruled.

It is somewhere to visit at that impressionable hour of late afternoon when the mind is most open to wonder, when the light falls in slanting bars through the window, piercing the shadows to fall on objects like none that one has ever seen before. And, if possible, it is a place to go alone.

Across the Avenue Jean XXIII, behind the wall against which the old woman sits with her bowl to await small gifts, is the museum of African art, its courtyard bowered by bending coco palms and great twisted trees that spread their shade over rampant but deliberate foliage. In back of the museum is a tract of grassless earth, also shaded, with a row of connected dwellings at the far end, forming a compound for the museum's staff, their families and their chickens.

Rooks croak in the upper branches. Lower down, bright little weaverbirds dart about, gathering straws to perfect their basket nests. On the ground, flightless roosters argue and strut and sharp-ribbed dogs sleep, while from the doors of the staff quarters come the voices of mothers scolding, babies complaining. Except in architecture, the compound behind the museum might be village Africa.

It is good to stand there a while, to let the sounds of the passing street soften and subside and to prepare one's thoughts for what waits inside.

Because the objects assembled in the museum's collection, things brought back by soldiers and merchants and missionaries from their penetrations of this part of Africa in an earlier time, are of a force to take the breath. The visitor is about to be convinced, if he ever doubted it, of the ability of wood to contain life—not just to represent life, or suggest it, but actually to *contain* it—long after being cut from the original tree.

The term "primitive art" is a pejorative shorthand that conveys no sensible meaning. The tools may be rudimentary. The materials may be the natural and often perishable ones that come to hand. But the method and the medium are essentially unimportant. For the expression of human genius has a sophistication that can vault any barrier of culture or time. As proof of that, one need only point to the cave paintings of Lascaux in France or Altamira in northern Spain.

Or to certain of the pieces that stand in the Dakar museum and hang on its walls.

Some of them are simple objects of the forest life. A drum, for example. The Senegalese are great and famous drummers. There is a drum in the museum that was fashioned from a single, whole log, perhaps three feet in diameter and six long. By introducing fire through a narrow slit cut in the top, the maker

Mask, private collection

Mask, Dakar museum

hollowed the entire log to an incredible thinness. Merely to rap the instrument with a finger is to start a thunder of sound rolling through the rooms of the building, growing in volume, deepening in its mellow pitch, until finally it rumbles away to a memory in the stillness of the mind.

A drum is all it is—but a stunning example of the technology of its time and place. A Stradivarius of a drum made by an artist.

Many of the masks are especially fine, sculpted by carvers whose solutions to representing the human features predated Cubism by a generation and more. Some of them are wryly humorous, others severe or even brutal and alarming. Often animal horns, bits of metal and bristling nails, human teeth, cloth, dried rushes or other materials are incorporated in the work. In no case is the result something crudely or accidentally arrived at. Each one is a product of originality and inspiration. It is plain the artist knew exactly the effect he wanted, and what's more, knew precisely how to achieve it. The most astonishing masks in the collection are from the Ivory Coast, in whose forests the art of carving seems greatly to have flowered.

There is much else of interest to be seen. But if the hour and the light and the mood are right, there is nothing more affecting than the two near-life-sized wooden grave guards that stand side by side in one of the museum's lower rooms. They are from Iboland in eastern Nigeria. You round a corner and there those two are waiting, armed with bows and spears and arrows in their quiver, staring directly at you out of eye sockets painted a luminous red.

The skin between the shoulders can be felt starting to crawl. A kind of startled hum sounds in the ears, and the failing light through the window seems somehow agitated where the figures stand. Something is alive in that room. Whatever those two are guarding, it's nothing any trespasser would be tempted to molest.

One comes out after that into what's left of afternoon, and

everything has changed. The city has changed. The people walking along its streets have changed. The streets themselves, and the cars that pass noisily by, seem temporary and insubstantial, oddly out of place. One understands better why Africa yields so uncertainly to being something different than the strange and powerful place it was.

The archaeological evidence suggests that human beings may have walked this continent before any other, chipped their first stone tools at the edge of its savannas, dreamed their first frightened dreams in the fastness of its darkling woods. There is something in the memory of Africa that blue jeans and transistor radios cannot touch—something that the younger races have forgotten how to remember, something to be trifled with only in disappointment and at possible peril.

12

ᴛHE FIRST SIGNAL OF CRISIS came in the form of a small squeak. The squeak sounded thin and mechanical, like the noise a gate might make, swinging in the wind on a rusted hinge. The American sat bolt upright in bed.

"There's something in the room with us," his wife whispered in a strangled way.

If she had said, "There's *someone* in the room with us," he would have been less alarmed. But some *thing*! What thing? In Africa—even in a settled part of it—that's not the kind of news you like to receive out of a sound sleep in the blind darkness of night.

He fantasized something large.

"What made that sound?" he said.

"What sound?"

"That squeak."

"I did," she said. "It's in bed with me."

That ruled out an elephant.

"It just crawled across my shoulder. Then through my hair."

He turned on the light and got up ready for a fight to the finish with the violator of his wife's bed. He saw nothing except the clock on the bed table that said half past 2 o'clock. The door was shut, the metal window shutters closed and bolted.

"Maybe it's under the pillow," he said. And sure enough, when he lifted the pillow the beast scuttered over the end of the bed, its slender tail disappearing last.

"It's just a lizard," he said.

"*Just!*" She gave a violent shudder, like someone racked by a fit of fever. "But it *crawled* on me."

"Uhhh," he said, being unable to sustain the pretense of heroic manliness for more than a few minutes at that hour of morning. He already was thinking of sleep.

"Look under the bed," she said.

He looked under the bed. Nothing. He lay down and immediately became unconscious of anything. When he woke in the first daylight, he found her wrapped up in the bedclothes like a mummy in its bindings, with only a breathing hole for her nose. That morning he mentioned it to the cook, Bocar.

"A lizard crawled over the madame in the night," he said, referring to her in a formal and impersonal way, as if to distance himself from the whole affair.

"A lizard!" the cook exclaimed. "In the bed? It isn't good."

"No. She didn't think so."

"What kind of lizard was it?"

"Like the one I saw go behind the cabinet in the kitchen the other day. I didn't see it too well, but I think it was the same kind."

He had expected Bocar to laugh, but instead the cook was taking the matter seriously.

"There are two kinds of lizards that can come in a house. One is the little salamander, like the one in the kitchen. He makes no trouble, that one. The other kind is the night lizard, and he is not good. He spits. And if he happens to spit on

A day lizard

someone, then that person is certain to become sick."

"How sick?"

"Not sick to die. But sick."

"Well, I don't think he spit on her. He just sort of crawled across. Probably it was only the salamander."

"Probably," the cook said.

The subject came up again at lunch.

"Bocar says there are two kinds of house lizards," he reported. "One is a harmless salamander. The other one is called the night lizard."

"It was night," she said.

Bocar was listening to the conversation as he served the fruit. "Yes," he said, "but the night lizard does not move much. He likes to stay on the ceiling or near the light fixture. Somewhere where it is warm."

"Like maybe the warmth of someone who is sleeping," the American said.

She didn't think that was funny. The cook prevented himself from laughing. In the afternoon, the American looked through the encyclopedia. On a hunch, he looked up *gecko*. The picture showed a fat-bodied, spotted creature with lidless eyes set in a wide, nasty-looking head. *The gecko is not venomous*, the encyclopedia entry said, *although in some regions it is feared and called "poison lizard."* He carried the book into the kitchen to show the picture to the cook.

"That's it!" Bocar said. "The night lizard. It's not pleasant, that beast."

Africa reveals her secrets slowly.

13

IN THE REGION OF CASAMANCE in the south of the country, and in Guinea beyond the frontier, the rains have begun. Also in Mali to the east, swelling the Niger River and spreading a miraculous carpet of green, travelers from there say, where only weeks ago there was not even a memory of burnt grass.

In dust and heat and expectation, Dakar and most of the rest of Senegal wait. But it is coming, the rain. You can feel it coming.

Last week the skies took on a different look, murky to the west out over the sea. Instead of rolling in long swells, the water danced and clashed in an irregular chop that made the fishermen of Soumbedioune hug closer to the coast in their wooden pirogues.

The wet winds blowing up from the equator to meet the dry breath of the harmattan exhaling southward out of the desert have begun to make a line of weather. What happens along that line in the weeks immediately ahead will mean, for hundreds of thousands of Sahelian people, the difference between plenty and much less than not enough.

The wet season used to begin here on the *Cap Vert* peninsula, in the country's middle climatic zone, reliably in mid-June. In the south it started even earlier, and in the north, up nearer the desert, was late and short. Then, in the late 1960s, toward the end of what was, for most of Africa, the first independent decade, the life-sustaining rains began to fail.

Change in the weather no more suggests the magnitude of what occurred than *cold snap* would describe the reglaciation of North America. What was beginning was a cycle of drought across Africa below the desert so horrific in its consequences for human beings and the land that, had it happened in some past millennium, it would surely have figured in the sacred legends of cults arising in that time. It has been, one might almost say, a Noah's Flood in reverse.

The rains failed one year, and countless marginal farmers and herders of the Sahel went hungry. They failed again, and people starved. Some years the rains started in a timely way—then abruptly stopped, letting the sun take everything. And the pattern was always, inexorably less. Season upon parched season the drought continued and deepened. Scrub rangeland became desert. Herds became caravans of bleached bones between dry waterholes. Whole areas larger than half the republics on Earth were simply emptied out—swept clean of life as surely as by any biblical inundation. Age-old relationships between man and the fragile environment were shattered beyond any reasonable hope of mending. And in their despair, refugees from this cataclysm swept down like locusts upon cities unprepared and unable to receive them.

Last year, in some of the worst-ravaged areas, the rains came again. Here in Senegal, they were the best in recent memory, beginning early, continuing late, falling like a benediction on a country that—with amazing civility, sustained by Africans' capacity for mute and fatalistic suffering—had endured the worst that Nature could deal.

But the memory of anything as terrible as that will not be expunged for generations, much less in a single beneficent year. And that is why people here study the sky with the intensity of castaways clinging to the floating wreckage and scanning the horizon for a ship.

"It rained again in Casamance," a man could be heard saying to another, as the two of them passed on the street.

"Yes, and it has rained in Conakry. And in Banjul."

"But only starting. Not yet regular."

"Next week, here, God willing. Or the week after."

And even as they spoke, already it was far on in July.

Today, toward the end of afternoon, a gusting wind rose from seaward. The sky darkened, and thunderheads began building—or what would be called thunderheads in any place of reasonable weather. All along the corniche, people could be seen standing, motionless, expectant, their dark figures silhouetted against the sea as it paled from ultramarine to polished gray.

The rain was so near you actually could smell it in the air.

Then, as they watched, the clouds rode away to westward. The wind fell. And the unwashed city settled for another night under the mantle of a year's dry dust.

14

LIKE THE WHITE HEAT OF A FORGE, the transforming power of all-consuming need is wonderful and terrible to see.

If the tide tumbles a shell onto the beach, someone will pluck it up, scratch a design on it and set out to sell it on the street. If the shell happens already to be broken, someone will crush it into smaller pieces and string those for a necklace. A crooked stick becomes a beggar's crutch, an empty plastic bottle a child's push toy.

The soles for the cheap sandals, like shower thongs, in which so many Africans are shod, are machine-stamped out of large plastic sheets. For miles in every direction from the factory, the cast-off sheets—perforated with endless identical footprints—find a new life strung together as fences for villages and their fields.

An empty cardboard box is not just trash. It becomes the indispensable tool of some small boy's living as a *porteur*, following behind shoppers at a market and carrying what they buy. Flattened, it may later become part of a house wall. Or it could be someone's bed.

Automobiles broken and abandoned at roadside all but disappear overnight, picked down to skeletons with every bit of fabric, glass and portable metal recycled for uses impossible even to guess.

Nothing is wasted. In the fire of desperation, everything is fuel. Even butterflies.

A length of string is tied to a slender stick, with a snippet of white paper attached to the end of the string to make a crude but effective lure. When the stick is waved, the scrap of paper twists and darts, and credulous butterflies are attracted to it, following it to the ground to be instantly pounced upon. Their colorful wings are then pulled off and glued to a sheet of paper—dozens, hundreds to the sheet—arranged to make a recognizable design. Vendors course the streets, turning page after page of these, until one wonders that there is a butterfly left alive anywhere in Africa. It is an art form born of impoverishment, repellent but undeniably ingenious in its way.

And not all the skills hammered sharp at poverty's forge are as bizarre as that. Some are the same talents valued in any society, except that here they are whetted to an almost miraculous degree. The art of tailoring, for example, which is exclusively a man's work, learned by apprentices at a young age and brought to high refinement in the open-fronted stalls along the maze of alleys in the Sandaga market and certain of the narrow streets leading off from it.

There, in poor light, at antiquated machines, the tailors sit usually in crowded rows of three or four, backs to the walls, facing each other across an aisle barely wide enough to allow a customer to enter. From morning until early evening, as long as they can see the stitches, they bend squinting over their work, enveloped entirely by an overwhelming clutter of fabric, washed round by heat and the ceaseless clamor and confusion from the street. Their gift at what they do is utterly amazing.

You have heard of actors who, after one quick reading of the script, could play their scenes to perfection. Or of musicians able to repeat exactly, or even improve upon, a complicated instrumental passage after just a single hearing. Such accomplishment usually is called genius.

Well, that's how the African tailors are with cloth. They work without a pattern, cutting and stitching entirely by eye. Show them some garment you want duplicated, or explain how you want it modified, or even draw on a scrap of paper what roughly you have in mind, and they will study it a moment, nod, shake out the folded material and bend to their work.

Every detail is fixed immediately in mind—every pleat and pocket, every belt loop and buttonhole, as well as the general effect that is wanted, even if what they have been asked to make resembles nothing they've ever seen. The customer is measured with the eye, and by a couple of quick passes with a frayed cloth tape. That is all.

It is a wonder to see—like Mickey Mantle in his heyday, swinging for the right-field fence, or Julius Erving airborne in the lane. There seems no deliberation in it at all, just pure gift. It is as if their eyes, their hands and the cloth itself were somehow united, without any intervening calculation, to translate an idea into reality by a process very near magic.

And they never err. *Never*. The garment always fits, always is exactly right. A simple assignment like coat and trousers or a lady's dress they will surely finish by the next midday. For something more ambitious—a queen's wedding gown, say— they might need until the day after.

They are proud of what they do, although they are paid very little for it. But it would not occur to them that their ability is in any way extraordinary. It is simply a craft, like any other, which they began learning as boys and have perfected through whole lives spent with their shoulders bent hard against the wheel of need.

Tailor on the Rue Paul Holle

Tailor's charcoal-heated iron

The American went to the market one day to pick up a jacket he'd ordered the afternoon before and stayed on several minutes in the suffocation of the shop, watching the row of tailors as they worked, the material flying effortlessly through their fingers. Anywhere else, he finally told one of them—in the States or in the great couturiers' salons of Europe—a talent like that could make a man rich.

The tailor looked up briefly, only half-believing, from his machine.

"How do I go there?" he said.

There wasn't any answer.

15

FAIRLY FREQUENT REFERENCE has been made here to the heat, but only in passing. The subject deserves treatment in its own right, because for something like seven months of every year heat is one of the main features—perhaps even the controlling fact—of life in this part of Africa.

Several days ago the electrical current in the house began to flicker and dim. Then the clothes washer refused to work. Then the refrigerator stopped cooling. Finally, and most catastrophically, the air conditioners one by one shut down.

The *toubab* has brought with him to the tropics his many gadgets. By the aid of all of them he is able to maintain a tolerable degree of comfort and even to forget, more or less, the true nature of the climate. But let those gadgets fail, and like some ferocious beast that lurks just outside the light-circle to await the dying of the fire, Africa comes rushing in.

There are hotter places than Dakar. *Much* hotter. Inland a couple of hours by car in the direction of Senegal's great central desert, the Ferlo, the thermometer in this season regularly climbs well above 100 degrees Fahrenheit. Farther east still, somewhere on the border between Senegal and Mali, lies a zone that some claim is the hottest inhabited place on the planet. One traveler spoke of passing through there at midday on the slow Dakar-to-Bamako train when the temperature was just a shade under 130, and you could tell from the way his eyes glazed over just talking about it that it was an adventure he will never forget—or, if he can help it, ever repeat.

Compared to that, the weather here on the coast is relatively moderate. But only *relatively*, and moderation is not to be confused with comfort. A daily temperature of around 90, with humidity of 99.9 percent—or whatever amount of water air can contain and still be breathable by creatures without gills—inevitably wears one down. For a stretch of days or several weeks even, one can endure. But when the prospect is for an unrelieved *half-year* of that, the spirit becomes enfeebled.

The *toubab*, who passes quickly from air conditioned bedroom to air conditioned car and thence to air conditioned office, manages to affect a style of crispness and vigor. Whereas the typical African is held to be lassitudinous, ill-motivated and slow moving. That is a malicious caricature—a product, almost certainly, of racist spite. But the slow moving part is true. The normal heat of Africa obliges everything to move slowly. Indeed, in all of Nature there may be no creature slower or more feckless than the *toubab* who has been deprived of his cooling appliances.

The rooms of the house fill up with steam. The bed at night becomes a rack of sleepless torment. One rises in the morning already exhausted and takes a tepid shower, but the mere effort of toweling off afterward produces rivers of perspiration. Fresh clothes are no help, because within minutes they hang like a clammy shroud, shapeless and noisome. Eye glasses hardly can be worn; water pools at their lower rims, or they slide off the wet bridge of the nose and fall on the floor and are broken.

Stinking and blind, the *toubab* stumbles about in misery and searches his fried brain for some recollection of what brought him to such a place.

There even is a distinct and recognizable method of locomotion in this climate, which some have called the African Slow Step. People afoot move as if walking at the bottom of a swimming pool, one foot placed ahead of the other with effort and deliberation while the arms make delicate little flipper-like gestures at the side. Between the hours of 10 o'clock in the morning and 5 in the afternoon, the progress between two fixed points of someone doing the African Slow Step is, like the movement of glaciers, detectable only by sensitive instruments.

During the electrical failure, it occurred to the American that he badly needed a haircut.

The first day he thought about it. The second day these thoughts crystalized into something like resolve. The third day, however, he remembered that the barber's shop lay an unimaginable distance away, four blocks at a minimum. By the fourth day he felt only a vague regret about being unable to get his hair cut. And soon after that he forgot it.

16

T HE MAN WHO GOES NAKED was seen the first time from the window of the car. He was walking in a throng of other people—among them, but not really one of them—in the early evening on the road beside the sea.

The others took no notice of him. They were just strolling along the pebbled roadside toward the city, all quite normally dressed except for the one man. In the failing light, the quick impression was of a tallish figure in a tight-fitting gray-black suit. The car rolled quickly past, and it was not until a second or two afterward that the startled mind actually acknowledged what the eye had seen.

The man was not wearing a stitch.

Several mornings later he lay fetally curled in his nakedness on the sidewalk outside the Roman Catholic cathedral. And the next day he was seen asleep on the searing pavement at the top of the Place de l'Indépendance. A week or so elapsed, then.

Yesterday he was met again, this time crossing at a signal light with a crowd of other pedestrians near the Sandaga

71

market. As before, the people in the jostle of the crosswalk paid him not the least attention. Without so much as a glance or a raised eyebrow, they just walked along at his side or toward and past him, some in animated conversations, others with eyes fixed straight ahead toward their destinations, registering no surprise. Their indifference added to the surrealism of the moment.

Dakar, it must be understood, is a city much like any other—better-off than some, poorer than many, but a regular city nevertheless, with certain conventions and rules of behavior to observe, one of which is wearing clothes. Senegalese of means are elegant dressers, and those of all classes are modest. Even the poorest cover themselves with rags.

All but this man.

He is of average height, his head either hairless or shaven, and appears to be in his 20s or early 30s. He does not look malnourished, nor does he seem to be a madman. At least he doesn't gibber to himself or roll his eyes with a crazy look. He has simply dispensed with clothes. A fine, gritty gray dust covers him entirely—face, arms, chest and all the rest—as if he had just come from a thousand-mile march across some parched and savage waste.

The total impression is spectral and somehow deeply disturbing.

Is his nakedness intended as a statement? A protest? Could it be that he is some kind of ascetic who has put off the troubles of the world and all its decorations? No one knows. No one seems able to explain. And in truth there may *not* be any reason other than, as someone speculated, he is simply *beyond the pale.* Meaning that he no longer considers himself a part of the society or perhaps even of humanity, and therefore honors no laws, is bound by no covenants, cares for nothing, even himself, and has achieved a state of final detachment.

If so, it is a terrible condition—most terrible of all to the orderly folk whose conventions become diminished and meaningless in the presence of a naked man.

Like a figment from a waking nightmare, he materializes suddenly out of the crowd, striding blank-faced and dusty and bare on the noonday street. Where he came from, where he is going, why he does it—all is mystery. The one thing sure about him is that he has nothing left to lose, and that's what makes the encounter so alarming.

17

JUST BEFORE 6 O'CLOCK in the dark of a morning like any other, a single rumble of thunder sounded. A pulse of sheet lightning ran whitely down the window. In the next instant, the lights in the hall and in the garden outside went off together.

And the rain came at last.

It arrived as rain ought to after a wait of nearly a year. Excessively, violently. The black sky opened to let the water drop in vertical sheets. In moments the air cooled, became almost chilly. The dark shapes of the nearest trees could be seen thrashing in the wind, but so huge was the weight of the deluge that no wind could deflect it. It fell straight down, beating on the house roof, beating on the pavement, pooling and rushing away in powerful freshets along the street.

From under the shelter of the broad eave came the voice of the night guard, conversing with someone in a joyous shout, his cries almost lost in the drumming of the water. By 7 o'clock the sky tried to lighten, but even at daybreak the far side of the garden could not be seen through the curtain of rain. For more than an hour it fell that way, the water running under doors and around windows, like an irresistible sea hunting out the weaknesses of a leaky ship. What must such a rain be, under a roof of grass thatch or corrugated tin? Or under no roof at all?

Then, suddenly as it began, it ended. The wind rushed away to somewhere else and left a cool but breathless quiet. The leaves, washed clean of their coating of reddish dust, reflected the light with an intensity that made the air itself a filtered green. And the first pedestrians came walking with a lighter, happier step.

The guard changed, and the American went outside in his pajamas to deliver to the gate man, Moussa, his coffee and his morning loaf.

"No electricity," the old man said with a delighted smile. "In the whole town, it's cut." Perhaps all his years spent in soldiers' field camps convinced him that cities have too much senseless complication, too much ease. He seemed very pleased that the current was off.

An hour after that, the pavement was almost dry. Where the water had briefly stood in considerable lakes, not even the smallest puddle could be seen. Like a traveler given refreshment after too long under a beating sun, the Earth had opened its parched throat and taken it all in one greedy gulp.

The lights came back on then. The gardener, Dialo, appeared on the walk, surveying his domain over which, this day, no sprinklers would need to turn. Moussa moved his folding chair out from under the eave. But the woman who begs outside the museum, faithless for the first time to her duty, did not come to sit against the wall. Evidently the start of the rains was gift enough.

18

𝒞HE COAST OF THE COUNTRY is broken in three places by great rivers emptying into the sea, although topography makes that description imprecise. So flat is the land that the rivers do not so much flow into the Atlantic as they simply *mingle* with it, rising and falling with the salty tides and therefore being of little use many miles inland except for fishing and limited transportation.

Farthest north, on the frontier with Mauritania, is the Senegal River, meeting the ocean at the former port capital of Saint-Louis. A bit more than midway down the coast, well south of Dakar, is the braided delta of the Saloum, with its many tributaries and miles of mangrove marshes and dark lagoons.

The southernmost is the Casamance River. And the region that straddles it—comprising roughly one-quarter of the country—is the one Senegalese generally consider to be the most beautiful in the republic, meaning that it is the wettest and the greenest. It also has the most mosquitoes. And inland even a short way from the sea, it is, in this season, very, very hot.

Actually, there is another great river, even vaster than the others, that cuts the coast between the Saloum and the Casamance, but it is not a river of Senegal. It is the Gambie River, lying in that sad illogicality of a nation to which the river gave its name—and properly so, since there is hardly anything else there worth mentioning.

The history of The Gambia can be told in few lines.

The British a couple of centuries ago coveted a foothold on this western bulge of Africa, a coast largely dominated by the Portuguese and French. After years of haggling, they managed to run up the Union Jack on an island at the mouth of the Gambie, and established there a settlement they called Bathurst. Just short of a hundred years ago, The Gambia became a crown colony whose boundaries, when eventually they were defined, contained only the river and some ten to fifteen miles of riverbank on either side. In this tiny, worm-shaped territory, surrounded entirely by Senegal except for the outlet at the sea, presumably Englishmen in white short pants and starched shirts played cribbage in the sweltering afternoons and cursed their miserable assignment.

Another seventy-some years elapsed before, in 1965, the British struck the colors and departed. But unlike the French, whose aim all along was to transplant a culture, the British left behind one modest town and very little else. The Gambia got a flag, a seat at the United Nations and all the other perquisites of statehood. What remains today of Bathurst, renamed Banjul, serves for little except as a decaying reminder of the long colonial folly.

But that's getting ahead of the story.

The early bus south from Dakar leaves at 9 o'clock each morning. Places cannot be reserved, so anyone who seriously plans to ride it is wise to be there well before 8, ready to rush on board and claim a seat. A minor official at the Gambian consular office, where visas had to be obtained in advance, made much of the machine's air-conditioned comfort. Be sure to take the

Gambian bus, he said, not a Senegalese one. Then he whispered his plea for money to fill the gas tank of his motor bike. The air conditioning turned out to be windows that, with some struggle, could be slid open.

Passing southward on the highway, a wash of green—faint at first, but growing more pronounced—gradually colors the landscape. Where only a week before there were gritty barrens, one rain has produced a show of life.

By a little after 2 o'clock the machine has crossed into The Gambia, and in a few more minutes has come to the river and the ferry landing. The ferry can be seen just leaving, which means a wait of three hours at blinding midafternoon in a tin-roofed shed smelling powerfully of urine. Among the waitees the money changers circulate, each one a private bank, trying to trade the worthless local currency for dollars, francs, Sterling, marks, yen—any sort of real money that can be spent in the outer world.

Because of the length of the journey to the south of Senegal and the bottleneck at the Gambian ferry, Banjul is the logical place to break the trip. Some travelers have even claimed to find it charming. When finally the river crossing is accomplished, Banjul at early evening is as beguiling as a sanitary landfill.

Incredible accumulations of refuse—broken and discarded things, and others organic and putrefying—wash up in chest-high waves against the walls of dilapidated buildings at the sides of once-paved streets that have simply crumbled away to red dirt. The people, too, are changed here. They have none of the animation or physical grace of the Senegalese. Gangs of idlers lounge in the dust and stare at the passing stranger with a look of sullen resentment—which is the expression anyone might have, if he contemplated a lifetime spent in such a place.

The street hustlers of Banjul, unlike those in Dakar, are worse than just clever and determined. They are intimidating and mean. They lay hold of a traveler, jerking at his arms,

maybe feeling for his pocket. One of them, when finally warned
.away in impatience, leaves with a threat.

"You will know the consequences of this later tonight," he
mutters. *"You will see me again!"*

It does get to be night, then. The Apollo Hotel, two blocks
from the ferry landing, proves an unfortunate choice. One
room has an air conditioner that works, but a toilet that does not.
In the other room, the air conditioner is broken but the toilet is
functional, though lacking a seat. By visiting the plumbing in
that room, and dragging mattresses through the hall to the floor
of the other, it is possible to imagine enduring the hours ahead.

Outside, on the small balcony, the temperature must be a
clammy 95 degrees. Across a confusion of shed roofs can be
seen only a few incandescent lights—so few that one is
reminded afresh of the miracle that electricity truly is. Figures
move in awful slow-motion through the dark trenches of the
dirt streets below. The refuse heaps sparkle wickedly in the hot
moonlight. The air is heavy with languor, with aimless fury,
with menace and defeat.

There are some errors of history, some human and political
deformities, that may be beyond the collective power or will of
international charity to correct. If so, this place is one of them.
Whatever was here before Banjul, before Bathurst—whatever
was here when *nothing* was here—was more than remains here
now of happiness or hope.

Mindful of that muttered threat, the travelers sleep fitfully
with a chair propped under the handle of the door.

19

IMAGINE A NETWORK OF PUBLIC TRANSPORT so far-flung that it could deliver riders to virtually any place in the country, even the smallest and most remote hamlet, over paved roads or barely passable back-country tracks.

Imagine that no reservations were required in advance, and that any sort of baggage, including live animals, would be accepted without complaint. Yet so flexible was this system that it offered not just one departure but many to each of hundreds of destinations every day, allowing travelers to leave at the time of their personal convenience.

Finally, imagine that the average cost of using this incredible means of transport amounted to only pennies per mile, meaning that almost any citizen could afford to ride.

Pure fantasy, you say. Out of the question, even for a highly developed country, much less a poor one. But such a network does exist here, created without a single World Bank study or a dime of foreign aid. Free enterprise did it all. And in its own incredible, fabulously chaotic way, the system works like a dream—so well, in fact, that no feasible alternative has ever been proposed.

It is the West African system of *taxis de brousse*, or bush taxis.

Quitting Banjul with gratitude at a still-dim hour of early morning, the travelers pass by ordinary cab to the "garage" at Sere Kounda, toward the friendly Senegalese frontier. What is called a garage actually is no structure at all, only a kind of open lot ringed by merchants' stalls, where something like a hundred vehicles of all imaginable descriptions are loading, departing, arriving in noisy but purposeful confusion. The machines range from antique minibuses to small-size pickup trucks with bench seats along either side of their metal-roofed beds, to still smaller French-built sedans, outfitted so that one person rides in front with the driver, three in the middle seat and three more behind.

Destinations are cried aloud by drivers and their assistants. Passengers are deftly corralled. The price is a fixed one, kept modest by unfettered competition. Money is paid, a ticket written out on a plain paper stub. No *taxi brousse* ever sets forth without its full complement of people inside and goats, pigs, sheep or chickens on top, but the wait generally is short. And the frantic activity of the scene is entertaining. Vendors hawk kola nuts, cashews, mangoes, soft drinks and candy. Beggars beg. Horns toot and car radios blare.

This morning there must be a half-dozen vehicles loading for Ziguinchor, the capital of Casamance Region, and the Americans fill out a load. It is one of the small trucks: Five riders to a side, one on a jump seat in the middle and two plus the driver up front in the cab. One of the passengers is taking a pig for his brother's wedding. The pig rides on the roof rack in a burlap bag, complaining bitterly, maybe guessing the journey can come to nothing good.

The road south passes into ever more verdant greenery, with oil palms and giant kapok trees soaring high over an understory of lower bush. From time to time a smallish, fox-red monkey can be seen loping across a clearing in the forest. The villages here have a neat, well-ordered look, with many bright roofs of new thatch.

There are endless police checkpoints along the way, with papers to be shown. Several years ago there was a brief uprising in this region, which thinks of itself as distinct from the rest of Senegal and resents the governance of the north. The police, the other riders say, are looking to be sure no guns are brought in. But the inspections are perfunctory. Wedding-bound pigs and families of sun-smitten *toubabs* do not look like the soldiers of tomorrow's revolution.

In early afternoon at the garage of Ziguinchor, the passengers of machines rolling in from every direction are again sorted and redistributed. A bank of gray clouds has risen up to cover the sky, but the air is still and breathless. Faint from the road, the pale travelers swill down bottled orange sodas, several each, cold from a vendor's ice chest.

This time the conveyance is one of the seven-place sedans. Just as it pulls out southwestward for the two-hour drive to the coast village of Diembéring, several large drops splash on the windshield, then the sky opens and the deluge comes. The driver hunches forward over the wheel. The passenger beside him wipes the fogging windshield with the flat of his hand.

The young man in the middle of the second seat is pleased that the Americans are going to the *campement* at his village. Many French people visit there in season—the season being the cool months of January through April. Also Germans and sometimes Italians or Spanish, but not often Americans. He writes his name, Pierre Badiane, on a piece of paper. He is 24 years old, of the Jola people, a Christian. Diembéring, he says, is a congenial mix of Muslims, Christians and animists. And it is a nice village. He would like to show the visitors through it, to introduce them to his family.

The visitors don't know about that, or about anything. They

Bush taxi loading, Ziguinchor

don't even know exactly what is a *campement,* except that someone recommended the one at Diembéring as being good. The car stops, unloads under an enormous kapok tree. They stagger with their duffels along a village path and up a hillside trail between the gnarled roots of more huge trees. They only know that they have gotten where they were going, whatever that turns out to be. The rain has nearly stopped. The light after the storm is luminous green. The air of the coming evening has been washed fresh and cool. And from a great distance, as they mount the trail, they can hear the soft rustle of the sea.

20

Τ HE CAMP IS SITUATED on a high, grassy knoll, the last prominence before the land falls away down a gentle slope of sand to the ocean's edge, where the long swells of the Atlantic come curling in upon an endless, gentle and utterly deserted shore.

For lodging there are grass-roofed, cement-floored huts, over which giant trees, survivors of the primal forest, spread their shade. Each hut has two cots, mosquito nets suspended from the ceiling, a small table, unscreened windows, a door. On the crest of the hill is a dining hall, also grass-roofed, with rough plank tables and benches. A little way below that stands a smaller building with a common shower and toilet. Those are all the amenities.

In every direction except seaward, the view from the hillock is down upon the rooftops of the village, which mostly are thatch with occasional sheet tin. People can be seen moving along the narrow pathways, and the dooryards of the houses are alive with children, chickens and the humorous little long-snouted pigs that frequently stray up—tidy creatures, fastidious and inoffensive as kittens—to munch the grass of the hilltop camp.

The men of Diembéring are fishermen and rice cultivators. In the morning, the boatmen take the path toward the sea, the farmers take another path inland toward their fields. The implements both carry are nearly identical—a stout pole hafted to a wooden paddle—but the one the *pêcheurs* shoulder is an oar for steering their pirogues, whereas the paddle of the farmers is rimmed with an iron blade for stirring the earth.

That much can be seen in the morning from the elevation of the camp. But little else.

The *campement* is an enterprise of several village men who went abroad to work in France and saved the capital for its construction. The government some years ago began encouraging the creation of many such camps, so that visitors, instead of passing from one European-style hotel to the next in splendid ignorance, might have a taste at least of country life. And it is a fine idea, because to know Africa at all, one has to know the sweetness of the village.

A long time back, in another West African country, the American and a party of geologists he was traveling with arrived on a narrow footpath through deep bush into a village much like this one, except smaller. Within minutes of their coming, the village chief sent a chicken for their supper. Afterward, they spoke with him in his compound, then slept on cots under the open sky, listening to the sounds of the place subsiding into sleep, staring into the fathomless depths of stars, hearing wild creatures cry in the night and waking at first light to the fog of the rain forest and the smell of breakfast fires.

Of all the memories of a long journey, that one remains among the freshest. But such opportunities are a matter of luck.

The luck this day is the young man, Pierre Badiane, who was their fellow passenger in the *taxi brousse* from Ziguinchor. He appears at the travelers' hut in midmorning and offers to show

The camp at Diembéring

them Diembéring. Another trail leads down from the hilltop into that pastoral world. And what seemed, from above, an impenetrable confusion can be seen now to have a perfect logic.

The dwellings and stables of the village, built of mud-clay brick with the thatch of bundled forest grass atop a conical scaffolding of branches, are laid out along a maze of connecting pathways between chest-high fences made of sticks, woven cane or palm fronds. Inside each fence is the unit of an extended family, with its little courtyard, its several houses, its animals and dooryard garden. In the shade of a house front two women are weaving baskets, not for tourists but for their own use. A man with one of the paddle tools is cutting a trench to rebuild his fence. Another woman is cleaning and bagging rice. Everywhere children are playing. Everywhere the strangers are met not with suspicion but with curiosity and friendly looks.

Besides the houses, Diembéring has a school, a youth center for dances, a mosque, a Catholic church, a small general store and a bakery, a blacksmith's forge, a village clinic—many of the ingredients, in other words, of a small country place anywhere in the world. Activity always is greatest in the early morning. By midday, as the weight of the heat bears down, the village sinks into the stuporous drowse of the tropics. Anyone who can takes shelter indoors, and even the animals that wander freely (though the ownership of each hen and piglet is known) gravitate to the shade of fence or tree.

During the afternoons, nothing can be seen to move, except the *toubabs* of the camp making their way down the slope of sand to the beach. The outlanders' habit of lying white and nearly naked, presenting themselves deliberately to the full vindictive force of the sun, must seem comical and a little crazy to people whose lives are arranged around avoiding such needless punishment.

But presently a breath of coolness stirs. The visitors climb back up the hill, shower themselves and wait for dinner to be

Night in the Casamance

called. The long-winged kites fly off to roost, and their place overhead is taken by squadrons of large fruit bats that come out at evening, twisting and squeaking through the blue air. Kerosene lamps flame softly inside the dining hall, and others are set out on the step for the campers to carry back to their huts.

The same lamps, all of them made in China, are lighted in the village, too. From up above, Diembéring no longer seems incomprehensible and strange. In the doorways of their houses, families can be seen gathered in the coolness, forms and faces in the lamplight. The sounds of talking, of laughter, of children singing and playing some hand-clapping game, float up to the hilltop. It is a hard life that's lived down there, but not a senseless or a sterile one. There is the comfort of families living close, wrapped in the larger security of so many others like themselves.

That is the texture of things shared and known that binds people to their village. It is the reason why Pierre, who has traveled, has seen the capital, says he will pass his lifetime here. And it occurs to the American that Diembéring is not so different, except in architecture, from the village where his own father grew up, thousands of miles away and more than eighty years ago. He feels, in the darkness, a sudden and powerful attachment to this place.

Then there is a stir at the door of the dining hall.

"To table!" the cook announces.

And the shadow of the campers—four French people, a Swiss and the Americans—can be seen moving against the light of the lanterns as they go in to find their places.

21

PIERRE, IT HAS BEEN LEARNED, has a new house. That is a happy discovery, since a new house was something the American had hoped to write about, mainly to prove a philosophical assumption which briefly stated was this: That although people may differ a good deal in their histories and habits, in the essential matters of their lives—of which shelter certainly is one—their wants must be everywhere much alike.

Thus it would seem that the African of the village must give forethought to the site where his dwelling was put; that in its construction, there must surely be improvisations on the customary pattern, individual touches of taste or craftsmanship that make the edifice in some way uniquely his own; that the building of it must be attended by some of the same sweet imaginings that a new house evokes in people of our culture.

Those are wonderfully appealing notions. Beguiling—*and all half-baked!*

Pierre, the last of seven sisters and brothers at home, hated always having to disturb his parents by knocking for admittance when he came home late, sometimes even as late as midnight, from dances in the village. He wanted a house, he said, "for my liberty"—one yearning, at least, which must be universal.

But where to put it, or where to put any house in Diembéring, was not a matter of discretion. Family ground is parceled out by the elected *chef* of that quarter of the village. Pierre asked his father for a piece of the family plot, and his father drew in the dust a rectangle measuring four steps by a little more than three.

Did he give much thought to his plan for construction?

Plan? Pierre was astonished by the question. Why, he built it as any other house in the village is built—as he supposes houses always have been built. Why would he make it any different? He began at the start of the dry season and finished three weeks later. From the edge of his father's garden he dug materials for the walls and floor. Mixing the sand and clay and water to the right consistency he remembers as the hardest part. The next hardest was cutting roof grass, which had to be carried from the forest several kilometers east.

Did he dream as he worked? Did he imagine ahead to his life in that new place?

Again, the question perplexed him. One dreams at night, he said, not while one is working. Sometimes at night he dreamed of mixing sand and clay with the water, but nothing more. When he had finished, he built a table and a bench—plain boards with legs—and a bed frame, also unadorned, to hold his sleeping mat. Two snapshots of his sisters on the wall, his mosquito net and his tin kerosene lantern exactly like the lanterns in all the houses completed his furnishings.

One day, in not many years, it was suggested, he will take a wife. And then will his house not be too small?

It will, he agreed. He'll have to ask his father for a larger space. Then he will destroy this house and build another in its place. A bigger one could take two months or even three to

Pierre (right) and his friend

make. That's how it always is done, Pierre said. Any house is a temporary thing.

Pierre and the American mounted together to the top of the dune and looked down on the village, from which the smoke of cooking fires rose in fine blue plumes. Among all the crowded rooftops, Pierre's house was, indeed, exactly like the others, only a bit smaller, its new thatch a bit brighter. The *sameness* was what most pleased him.

Societies organize themselves around different wants and expectations. It seemed clear, in that moment, that the idea of a house as a work of individuality and relative permanence, a statement of oneself, is an odd and by no means general conceit. For all that we are brothers, men everywhere are far from being all alike.

22

T HE QUESTION UNDER DISCUSSION was a crucial one: How best to make one's way from the south of the country, across the intervening territory of The Gambia and back to Dakar, without being subjected a second time to the unpleasantness of Banjul.

These important deliberations were taking place at the beach, and the travelers' friend, Pierre, had come to sit with them under the thatched sunshade, this being their last afternoon. The sky was high and cloudless, the ocean an astonishing blue. Crabs scuttered in and out of their holes, and formations of little shore birds advanced and retreated, quick-footed and important, with the lapping and receding waves.

The map showed an alternate route, swinging in a wide arc east and north and crossing The Gambia at one of its narrowest points, where that country is hardly more than 15 miles wide. But that way would be longer, and might lengthen the trip by a day. Also, the river ferry was said to be often broken, and at its best even slower than the one at Banjul.

Difficult choices. But Pierre had a thought.

"It is possible to go by boat from Ziguinchor to Dakar," he said. "The boat travels down the Casamance River and then up the coast to the capital. It is called the Dakar Express."

The idea of a boat ride immediately caught their interest— just to get on board and be borne on the water and be delivered in perfect leisure to the port of Dakar, without ferry crossings or the countless stops for police checks. How effortless and inviting that sounded.

"You may take a private cabin, if you like," Pierre said. "Or you can simply have seats. As you prefer."

They discussed it. Who would want to travel up the coast of Africa shut away in the isolation of a stateroom? Regular seats would be fine. Or, even better, deck chairs if those were available. A cabin, it was agreed, would only be a senseless extravagance.

"Anyway," said Pierre, "it is an easy journey. Five hours at most, and you are there."

And when did the boat leave from Ziguinchor?

"On Saturday," their friend said. "In the middle of the day. You must depart from here by bush taxi at 7 o'clock in the morning. Before 9 o'clock you are in Ziguinchor, and you visit the market. It is a fine market, with many unusual things to see. And then, after two or three hours, you take the boat and you are in Dakar at 5 o'clock or 5:30 in the afternoon."

Yes, Saturday would be just splendid. And while they were in the market at Ziguinchor they would buy a basket and pack a picnic for the afternoon on the boat. They talked about what they should take.

Maybe a smoked chicken if they could find one. And certainly a loaf of bread, and fruits that could be peeled for their stomachs' sake. Bananas were not a good choice, because if they were ripe and then carried in the heat they would not do well. Oranges, in that case. And probably they should take bottled water. Or did Pierre think it might be possible to get cold sodas on the boat?

"On the Dakar Express," he told them, "it is possible to have anything. There is even a restaurant with tables, although it would be pleasant and less expensive to take one's own food along."

So, it was settled then. They would stay an extra day, either here or overnight in Ziguinchor, and still be home on Saturday as they'd planned. Without being covered with the grime of the road. Without the scorching wait of several hours at the river. There are only a few fit ways to get anywhere. Good trains are one, but ships surely are the best.

All that remained was the issue of how passage could be booked, since neither the *campement* where the travelers were staying nor the village of Diembéring itself had telephone service. Perhaps a message could somehow be sent to Ziguinchor this very day. Or did Pierre suppose, with the heat and the rain in the south and so few tourists on the move, that advance reservations might not be necessary?

What was his advice in the matter?

"Usually it is better to reserve," he said. "However, unfortunately, just now the boat is *en panne.*"

They couldn't believe they had heard him right.

"It's *what?*"

"Yes, it's a pity. The boat was broken several months ago and has been taken to Dakar for repair," Pierre told them. "Maybe it will run again someday."

And so their thoughts turned numbly forward to the wait at the ferry, which at the latest report was four hours—with any luck.

23

*T*HE APPROACH TO THE LANDING IS signified by a quarter-mile-long line of parked trucks, tractor-trailers and big flat-bed rigs far down on their springs under loads of immense logs and bagged peanuts and rice from the south of Senegal, all trying to make their way across the Gambie River to markets in the north.

It is not encouraging to see that the drivers have slung hammocks under the trucks and set up housekeeping there in the shade of their machines, with stoves and cooking vessels—a regular camp. Some of them have been waiting as long as three days for a place on the ferry. Waits of a week and more are not unheard of.

The river here flows slow and smooth between its mud banks, the distance across it not much greater than the length of the line of trucks. One of the two ferries is out of order and in fact is roped to the quay in what looks to be a terminal state of dereliction. But even the availability of only a single boat cannot begin to explain such a bottleneck.

Stalled at the Gambia ferry

Fish seller at the ferry landing

The obvious solution, of course, would be a bridge. But there is no money to build one, and the Gambians—all 700,000 of them—are said not particularly to want one. Commerce and travelers would only speed quickly through and on. It would be, they fear, the first step toward economic and ultimately perhaps even political integration with Senegal. The Gambians would rather preserve the fiction of nationhood, in a territory smaller than Connecticut with an economy based mainly on foreign gifts, smuggling and inconvenience.

Hence the wait at the river, on whose banks a dismal market has grown up to mulct the disconsolate travelers while they sit stewing in the endless line.

The merchandise in all the little shed stores is identical, and peculiar to say the least. The Gambia appears to have cornered the world supply of Ovaltine and Italian processed tomatoes, sold in cans ranging from ordinary small tins to containers as big as pails. Also there are banana creme sandwich cookies from England, limp as noodles in the moist climate, and incredible mountains of peppermint toothpaste and Palmolive soap. How the merchants came by all these treasures it probably is better not to ask. The only items of real interest are the bottled orange sodas from vendors' ice chests.

The Americans later reckon that, between them, they have drunk 17 bottles of the stuff during the interminable afternoon—enough to turn their saliva to orange syrup.

The filth and the heat at the treeless landing are indescribable. The sole sanitary facility is a rickety structure elevated on stilts and overhanging the river, so that disposal is by gravity directly into the stream. A few yards from that a man can be seen washing his hands fastidiously at the water's edge. Presently a fisherman arrives in a pirogue, eviscerates his catch there and sells the fish on the spot. A bit after that, another man crouches at the same place to wash his tin dinner plate, knife and spoon.

101

The only thing slower than the sun's blinding progress across the sky is the ferry in its occasional sorties back and forth across the river, with unexplained interruptions of an hour and more between. Meantime, an armed soldier circulates among the marooned crowds, warning that no photographs may be taken—"for security reasons." When asked *Security against what?* he flies into a rage.

Some African travelers give up the wait, traversing the river in fishermen's canoes and taking their chances on finding transport at the other side. The single encouragement is that passenger cars are being given priority, with only one of the big trucks loaded on board for each crossing. At that rate, it could be next year before rice from Casamance reaches the cooking pots of the north.

Twilight begins gathering over the river. Men set up charcoal braziers beside the line of cars to grill skewered mutton for sale to the stalled caravan. The trays of uncooked meat are black with a living rind of flies. Before hunger drives the Americans to that, their bush taxi rolls onto the ferry. The crossing itself is quickly accomplished, and after four and one-half hours they speed past the Ovaltine suburb on the far bank and are delivered from the purgatory of The Gambia.

In darkness, with windows open to let in the rush of wind, the car cools. Then the lights of Kaolack, the pleasant capital of Sine Saloum Region, shine in the night ahead. The Hôtel de Paris has vacancies. Its rooms are spotless. A shower washes away the crust of a week's back-country journeying.

Like soldiers newly returned from the front, the travelers feel a sense of well-being that is abnormally intense. Repeated little shudders of happiness pass over them. Within minutes, they are bent over plates of boiled shrimp in the open courtyard restaurant. A fresh breeze flutters the table linen. So vast is their gratitude that they might easily weep.

24

Т HE FRENCH, WHEN DAKAR WAS THEIRS, called it the Paris of West Africa. At first look, the comparison is absurd. But to return here after a week's hard traveling away is to see the place with a different eye.

A friend describes the arrival back in a large African capital, this or any other, as like coming out of a tunnel, especially if the return is at night. For hours on end one plunges ahead through the dark. A curious unreality captures the mind—a sense that time is meaningless, distances unmeasurable, and that one's destination may itself be a fiction.

Then, low in the sky, a premonitory glow rises. And minutes later one is flung out of the dark tunnel across centuries and into light: Streetlamps shining; buildings with their windows all ablaze—buildings that may in fact be quite ordinary, but which suddenly seem very grand. There is a sense that one has been impossibly far away from anything, and that by luck and providence has been miraculously enabled to come home.

That, at least, is the sensation for a Westerner, though an

African's feeling may not be the same. And it lasts for several days. The uncleanliness and the deterioration are less notice-able. One sees instead the broadness of the avenues of over-hanging trees, the flowers blooming in the traffic circles and public squares, the variety of architecture after the relentless sameness of the village.

How could one ever have imagined the city as lassitudinous and threadbare? People walk quickly by in a rush of color and vitality and purpose. Newspaper vendors hawk the day's headlines at every stoplight. A sudden blare of sirens announces the passage of a motorcade of dignitaries, riding like shadows of power behind the tinted glass of their limousines. Shop win-dows are full of enticing things. Airline billboards proclaim the nearness of Europe. People take their ease at tables under cafe awnings. Even the traditional markets, with all their clamor and seething confusion, seem somehow manageable and even cosmopolitan in their way.

That is the difference several days up-country can make. The change, of course, is not in the city but in the beholder. He feels at home there in a way he did not before, simply because, alien as the place may be, he comprehends now how much *less alien* it is than all the places that lie beyond. And there is the kernel of a real problem, which is that cities like this one have almost nothing to do with the reality or the truth of Africa.

Dakar is an invention of the French, just as Nairobi, on the continent's far side, is a relic of British conceit. Cities are where governments sit, where information is more or less controlled, where power is brokered and deals are made, where foreign deputations call briefly to distribute their largesse, where the clever and the well-connected few become incredibly rich. But Africa's future will not be decided in the capitals.

Yesterday, the president of Senegal came back to Dakar from Addis Ababa, in Ethiopia, where several days earlier he had given a valedictory address at the end of his term as head of the

Organization of African Unity. Ethiopia is a charnel house, and there is, if anything, *less* unity in Africa now than when the OAU was formed in the early years of independence nearly a quarter-century ago. But forms must be preserved. The presidential guard was resplendent in its scarlet uniforms, and crowds of citizens had gathered to welcome the leader back to his palace overlooking the sea.

It can be stated with fair certainty that, outside the capital and a few other settled places, none of this will have received much notice—the going or coming from Addis Ababa, or anything that was said there. For it has little to do with those Africans, which is to say *most* of them, who understand nothing of politics and even less of affairs of state, and whose immediate concern is only the withering of their fields under a rainless sky.

Yet it is there, in the alien countryside, that the battle for the future will have to be fought. Either the agrarian peasantry will be awakened out of its long sleep of neglect and powerlessness or else the cities, with their swollen bureaucracies and the insatiable claims of the elite, will continue to soak up the few resources like a sponge, and Africa will sink away beyond rescue into hunger and self-devouring rage.

At this point in its history, with numbers growing and need so great and time so short, there looks to be no middle ground.

Dakar street, morning

A colonial house

Laundry cooperative, Dakar

Flower lady, Kermel market

Cloth merchant, Sandaga market

The ubiquitous burger

Mauritanian silver market, Dakar

The silver-worker's boy

25

THERE IS A LIMIT TO HOW MUCH anyone needs, or wants, to know about the Guinea worm.

The creature is said to enter the body at some vulnerable spot, such as the soft flesh between the toes. Having taken up residence, it thrives, grows and migrates, finally making its presence known by a boil-like eruption somewhere on the outer skin. When the lesion is opened, the head of the worm can be seen.

That is the bearable part. What follows is worse.

The worm has to be extracted, which is done by wrapping its foreparts around a stick and rolling the stick to draw the thing out a few centimeters or inches at a time. Patience is called for, as the process may take several days.

Meanwhile, the stick must remain attached, either until the parasite is entirely removed or the victim goes mad with disgust, since to break off a Guinea worm during the course of extraction is said to cause even worse complications—if anything worse can be imagined.

114

That is one of the little joys of the tropics. There are others, although none quite so dramatic.

It is paradoxical that the same season upon which this zone of Africa depends to refresh the earth, to start crops greening and ultimately to sustain life, should bring with it so many problems of health. *Hivernage*, the wet time is called. The air is muggy. In the hothouse climate, germs and fungi and things that creep are roused from dormancy, multiply and begin their assault.

For example, Dakar these last few weeks has been swept by an epidemic of pinkeye, which the Senegalese call *Apollo*, since the first known case of it here occurred after one of the U.S. moon flights and it is suspected that the return of the rocket and the onset of the disease may in some way be connected.

The cook, Bocar, was out part of last week with malaria, which always bothers him when the rains begin and which this time was compounded by some kind of racking bronchial infection. The beggar lady across the street missed several days at her station outside the museum, felled by the *grippe*. This was reported by the gate guard, Moussa, whose stiffness in the shoulders and neck finally obliged him to visit the doctor when he could no longer turn his head.

Mosquitoes hatch by the millions. Bugs crawl. Raised by the wind, infected dust circulates. In every puddle, some eager nastiness awaits its host. The great heat has caused an invasion of night lizards, evidently seeking comfort in the house.

One recent evening a picture moved on a bedroom wall, and an odd clicking noise could be heard coming from behind it. As the picture was being taken down, a night lizard rushed horizontally across the wall on suction-toed feet, dodging the blows of a tennis racket. When finally caught, it released its fat tail, which still wriggled with great vitality. Lizard and tail both were carried out to the garden, where the night guard fell upon them with his club.

But that only accounts for one. There are three others, at

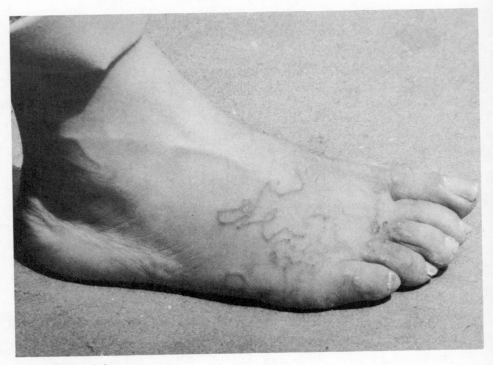

An inhabited foot

least—a large one somewhere in the living room drapes, a medium one in the hallway, a small one on the wall of the garage. Never mind that books say they are harmless. During *hivernage*, there is danger everywhere. And reasonable or not, the terror of the Africans—who live here, after all, and *ought* to know—communicates itself powerfully to the Western mind.

As if that were not enough, the American yesterday discovered what appears to be a worm in his foot. The top of the foot is inflamed, and the skin is raised in a pattern of threadlike whorls that very much suggests something alive just underneath. He has been advised to see a doctor, which he certainly intends to do. He is praying that it can be driven out of him with a pill and has already decided that if by some chance it is the Guinea worm, he is going to have himself put under general anesthesia for as long as it takes to get it out, because that business with the stick is something no one should be asked to do awake.

Dakar itself so far has had but two rains and one brief sprinkle. The crops of the region already are in serious distress, and more is desperately needed. But rain, as you see, is not an unmixed blessing.

26

THE CONTEST BETWEEN PRESENT tranquil beauty and the remembered agonies of the past, competing for possession of one's senses on the self-same piece of hallowed ground, can deeply confuse the mind.

That happens on certain historic battlefields, where the screams of nameless soldiers blown apart and dying still ring horribly across the perfect lawns and neat, wooded groves of a terrain long since given over to bronze markers along paths laid out for the padding feet of the curious. It happens in the congenial little square of the French city of Rouen, where Joan of Arc was burned to please the English and her enemies in the Church.

And it happens most certainly on the tiny Isle of Gorée, a thirty-nine-acre outcrop of sand and hard, black rock just twenty minutes by a small passenger ferry off the coast of Dakar. *"The strangest disease that I have seen,"* David Livingstone, the British missionary and great explorer of Africa once wrote, *"seems really to be broken-heartedness, and it attacks free men who have been captured and made slaves."* On Gorée island, nearly a century and one-half since the last slave ship hoisted sail bound for the Americas, the lingering miasma of the disease still breathes from the very stones.

Gorée's history is long—longer by a good deal than the story of European settlement in Senegal itself. In the middle 1400s, Portuguese navigators prospecting down the continent's west coast came upon the island, with its sheltered anchorage, and claimed it for their own. But the claim was only as strong as the cannons that enforced it. The Dutch, too, had African ambitions, and by the early 1600s Gorée was theirs.

In those first years, the island was civilization's outpost on this stretch of coast—the rest being only the pagan shore seen murkily across two miles of intervening water. It was not until 1638 that French merchants founded a trading settlement they called Saint-Louis at the mouth of the Senegal River to the north, and two centuries more before the building of a fort in 1857 on the mainland facing Gorée heralded the establishment of the town of Dakar. After the Portuguese and Dutch were driven from the field, France and Britain contended bitterly for possession of the island.

During two hundred years, under frequently changing European masters, Gorée's chief export was human beings. Captured in the interior by raiding parties of collaborating tribes, these unfortunates were delivered to the island and held there to await out-loading on ships bound west across the Atlantic. Some 60,000 are thought to have made that brokenhearted journey from Gorée.

In sheer numbers, the traffic did not approach that conducted out of Africa to the east by Arab slavers to Persia, Arabia and India, or from the so-called "Slave Coast" along the Gulf of Guinea, farther south around Africa's western bulge. But numbers are in a sense irrelevant, since they neither describe nor quantify suffering. And nowhere have the relics of that evil time been better preserved than on this small island.

In the *Maison des Esclaves*, an example of one of the many slave houses operated by rich merchants and the trading

119

companies, one can climb to the airy upper rooms where the traders lived and kept their accounts, and after that descend to the fetid stone-and-masonry holding cells where the "inventory" in that wretched commerce passed their last days and weeks before their journey. The iron rings for the chains still are in the wall. The light filters in weakly through slit windows. And the view from none of those windows is back toward Africa. The single perspective they give is of a vertical snippet of sky above and of waves pounding relentlessly upon broken rocks below. Between is only the sea—running off in distance and unknown danger to that other place, from which there could be no hope of return.

It is powerfully affecting just to spend quiet time there and to imagine.

The Isle of Gorée is a shrine, and the restored *Maison des Esclaves* its holiest artifact. On the walls of the open courtyard are placards bearing commemorative quotations. One, by Leopold Senghor, the political father of modern Senegal, reads: *No! You are not dead for nothing. You are the witnesses of immortal Africa.* Also displayed are photographs of many African heads of state and of notable black pilgrims—among them, the musician Stevie Wonder and Alex Haley, author of *Roots*—whose sense of history or reverent obligation has drawn them to this place.

One wonders what some of those visitors must experience in the encounter, especially black Americans and black Europeans of influence and accomplishment.

Beyond doubt, the slave trade was an inhuman business. Its immediate effects on the victims and on the continent were monstrous. But what thoughts now assail the far descendants of people taken in bondage so long ago from Africa's shore and who survived the passage and all that followed, eventually to seed new countries with free men boldly dreaming? Would they *really* undo history? Would they exchange the lives they

120

Gorée Island footpath

The slave house

have won for lives led in the hopelessness and squalor and plain political brutality of much of today's Africa?

Probably the question cannot be asked, or even the most honest heart be commanded truly to answer it.

Gorée's centuries of importance are long behind. Emptied by plagues and by the shift of administration and commerce to the mainland, it is home now to but a few hundred souls, many of them of families with generations' residence on the island. There is a small hotel, a terrace restaurant that overlooks the ferry mooring and the sea, a scrap of beach where day visitors take the sun, relic fortresses and, between the antique houses, narrow footways bowered by flowering vines. One sees at every turn some remnant of capricious architecture and exotic charm. And though all is in relentless deterioration, with stones falling and walls cracking, there remains a sense of ruined elegance.

Then evening comes, and the day people go back on the ferry to Dakar. The risen moon flings an avenue of splintered light across the Bay of Hann, shining whitely even through slit windows into the darkness of the slave house. Silence wraps everything, agitated only by the rush of wave on stone, and the island is left to its memories and few residents.

As old buildings fall and others are bought up for restoration by outsiders, the authentic population of Gorée is progressively displaced. It is even rumored that certain interests would prefer to see the island emptied of all its poorer residents and built up with luxury hotels, pricey eateries and fancy shops, so that tomorrow's pilgrims might dispose of their travelers' checks in maximum comfort, without being dismayed by any of Africa's more intimate odors or inconveniences.

Commercialism is the first rule of our times, and history a commodity like any other. After all, does not the restaurant in the village outside the death camp of Auschwitz, Poland, do a handsome tourist business?

27

AFRICA IS NO PLACE to have insomnia. The darkness is too vast, the silence too final. There is nothing to deflect the images that come crowding in.

In all his life the American cannot remember a half-dozen restless nights. But now, with a tooth going bad in his head and the worm still working in his foot, he finds that sleep will not come. Tired, he sits on the edge of the bed nearest the window and waits to be tireder. Until sometime after 1 o'clock occasional cars go past on the street below, their headlights briefly reflecting in the room, their tires sounding sticky-wet on the hot pavement.

Then the cars stop. And the transistor radio of the night guard goes off down at the corner of the garden by the gate, meaning that the guard is asleep in his chair. No moon or stars can be seen through the window. The wind-up alarm clock on the table beside the bed makes a metallic tick. The American sits owlishly awake on the edge of the bed and cannot even for a minute stop thinking, though the thoughts are patternless and confused.

He remembers being hit on the head in the street outside the Sandaga market—a blow that surprised more than it pained, struck from behind without reason or warning. When he turned, the man had glared at him for an instant, then walked quickly on. *"Fou,"* the market people had declared. A crazy man. And probably it was so, although in that brutal face he had seen a lucid and deliberate fury.

He thinks of the leper outside the bakery on the Boulevard de la République, hurrying to show his gray fingerless hands to people coming out with their sacks of morning sweets.

It gets to be nearly 3 o'clock. A dark figure passes alone on the street. The scuffing footsteps recede.

He thinks of the cook, Bocar, who left once to work in France and whose child sickened and died while he was away; who imagines that if he had only been here he might somehow have prevented it, and who never will leave again because he believes now that distance is dangerous.

And maybe it *is* dangerous, the American thinks, feeling incredibly far from any place he knows.

He is mystified by the inability to sleep. The tooth does not hurt very much, and the discomfort of the worm is mainly the disgust of thinking about it. The trouble must be something else. But without sleep it will be impossible to do any work in the morning, so he lies on the bed and tries, without luck, to forget where he is and what is outside the house.

He thinks of the leper, the face of the crazy man, his worm, the cook's dead child. He sits up again on the edge of the bed, wishing a car would go by or the guard would turn his radio back on. The clock ticks noisily and its faintly-glowing hands say that there are three hours, still, before any light.

28

ETIENNE IS A TALL, studious young man of 25, who has finished, successfully, his next-to-last year's examinations at the university. The new term does not begin until November, and meanwhile there is no work to be found. So when he happens to be passing in the neighborhood he occasionally drops in unannounced to sit an hour and practice his English.

His tendency to long silences gives to these conversations a disconcerting dreamlike quality. Small talk does not interest him. Between exchanges, he is content to wait for minutes at a time, his eyes behind wire-rimmed glasses fixed unblinking on the wall of the room or even somewhere beyond.

"The trouble," he said yesterday, after one of those spells of silent gazing, "is not *now*." Etienne's English is good, but his voice is so soft that you must almost lean to hear him.

"The trouble is later, when one finishes at the university and comes out with his certificate and finds there is no job." Silence. "Some man who is not even trained, but who has the right connections—he will have the job." Longer silence. "But you,

you might wait for five years to have one."

Etienne stared off at the wall through his glasses.

"I have friends who say, *'You are wasting your time to study. Why do you bother with it? What good will it do?'* They just stay all the day in their beds. They say, *'I have an uncle in one of the ministries. He will find me a place, maybe tomorrow.'* They only worry to find something to eat today, and if they find it they say, *'Well, all right, today is provided for and tomorrow may be better.'* Tomorrow. Always tomorrow! And while they wait they are getting old."

It was a long speech for him, and what seemed an eternity elapsed before he whispered, with an angry sigh, "This country!" Then was still again.

It was a sad situation, one had to agree. But it seemed to be how things worked here, and what could be done to change it?

He replied without taking his eyes from the wall.

"Revolution."

He said it flatly, impassively. As if it were just a word like any other, without special importance. "The problem is that no one wants to die, and in a revolution people die."

Perhaps, then, it could be a quiet revolution, the American suggested—an *intellectual revolution*, to repeat a phrase he had heard one of the university professors, a historian, use at a luncheon table several days before.

Etienne considered that for some minutes, then shook his head.

"No," he said. "Most of the country is not educated. The peasant—" He pronounced it *pay-sant.* "The pay-sant believes only what he is told. If he has millet to eat, and it need not be much, just a little, then life is all right. If he is hungry, next year could be better, *inshallah*—if God wills it. He has paradise to look forward to. So he prays and does what his *marabout* tells him, and the *marabouts* do not want revolution. They like it as it is now.

"Even our parents cannot understand," said Etienne. "If we students try to make a strike, they say we are crazy because the government has all the power, which is true. It has the army, the police, the gendarmerie. It has the radio, which is very important because people think that everything that comes on the radio must be true. If we make a strike for a real reason, then the radio says, *'They are just lazy and do not want to go to their classes.'* And our parents tell us to stop making foolish trouble. What can you do if even your own parents are against you?"

These discouragements struck him silent again.

"So I don't know if there will be a revolution or not," he said finally. "I think it is the only way, but who can know if it will come?" His voice took on a sudden vehemence. "I do know this. I will not spend five or ten years waiting for tomorrow! I will go out to someplace else. People say it is too hard to leave one's own home, one's family. So for that they stay, and lose their chance. But not me. If there is nothing for me here, then I will go out. It is my plan."

It seemed pointless to ask, *Go out to where? Go out to what?* At age 25, it is easy to imagine one's control over such things. He seemed heartened by his declaration of purpose. And after staring silently at the wall for another three or four minutes, he rose without a further word and left to find some way to pass one more pointless day.

29

A WHISTLE SHRILLED. The policeman waved the car to the curb. He approached the window, saluted, and said, "You passed through that red light. May I see your car's papers. And also your permit to drive."

He was a slender officer with a small, well-trimmed mustache—very natty in his tan uniform and extremely polite. The documents were delivered up. The policeman studied them, and found them to be in order.

"So," he said. "I am keeping these. You may have them back when you come tomorrow morning to the *préfecture* of police."

The American's heart sank. Tomorrow morning would be difficult, he explained. He had planned to go fishing, and had arranged for a pirogue at the village of Yoff. If he had to go to the *préfecture*, the boatman would lose a day's wages and he, the American, would be deprived of the chance to fish.

"It's a bad situation," the policeman agreed. "Maybe we should have a drink together and discuss it." Leaving his post at the intersection, he led the way down a side street, around a corner and into a little Arab stall.

"A Fanta," the policeman told the Arab.

"Two Fantas," the American said. The Arab set the cold bottles on the counter top. The American paid, and slid one of the orange drinks to the officer who, at the same time, slid back to him his driver's license and registration papers. Companionable as old friends, they stood in the shade of the stall and drank their pops, which were welcome refreshment on a sweltering day.

"Now . . ." said the policeman, when they had emptied their bottles.

The American withdrew from his pocket a 500-franc bill, worth about $1.50. He looked at the policeman, who was looking at the banknote with sadness. The American put it back in his pocket and took out a 1,000-franc one instead. He folded the bill small and passed it discreetly to the officer.

"*Un cadeau!*"—a gift—said the policeman, evidently pleased.

The American expressed gratitude at being able to go fishing tomorrow, after all.

"We like to help foreigners whenever possible," the officer said. "Think of me when you are in the pirogue."

The American promised he would. And he did.

30

*T*HE SEA UNDER A MURKY EARLY morning sky runs in long, smooth swells toward the mainland, hardly more than a dark shadow low on the horizon three miles to eastward.

Lines are out behind, and the boatman, Ouzin, adjusts the speed of the outboard motor to keep the baitfish just skipping nicely on the surface. Other boats can be seen at a distance, all of them the canoes of African fishermen, bobbing into view for a moment atop the swells, then disappearing again in the troughs between.

The season has been a good one, and the morning is right. It should be a perfect day, Ouzin thinks, to hunt the *espadon*.

The Atlantic sailfish is a magnificent creature, a prize so sought after, an adversary so worthy, that otherwise-rational men have been known cheerfully to bankrupt themselves and wreck their marriages in pursuit of it. To begin with, it is a game fish of great size and agility, reaching a length of six feet or more and weighing well over a hundred pounds. Its courage when taken on tackle of suitable weight is matched by its ferocious strength. And if that were not enough, it is an animal of stunning beauty, with its rapier bill and its fanlike dorsal sail and, when still alive in the water, brilliant coloration in shades of silver and purple and blue.

The current that rounds the coast of Africa here is rich in marine life of all sorts, but is notable for the great seasonal runs of sailfish beginning in June and continuing into September. Something like half of the world rod-and-reel records for the species are owned by sportsmen out of Dakar. There are people, especially French people, who have arranged their careers at some professional sacrifice just to live here and fish the *espadon*.

It is an expensive amusement. A day's hire of one of the big Air Afrique charter boats out of the Dakar marina runs 140,000 Senegalese francs. And if anyone bothers to ask, that price—the equivalent of about $400—does not include lunch. But some of the seriously addicted have decided there is a better way.

For as long as there have been dwellers on this shore, they have looked for sustenance to the sea. In their traditional pirogues, fishermen have ventured far out on every day of reasonable weather—and on some days not so reasonable—to live by their wits and the luck of the catch. They were doing it when the first Europeans set eyes on the African coast, and they do it still, the technology of their occupation little changed except for the availability of manufactured lines and hooks, and the ubiquitous Japanese-made outboard motor.

These local fishermen are not long on technique. It's meat they're out for, not the sport. They fish with heavy handlines, two hundred pounds breaking strength and greater. On their fingers they wear rubber guards for protection and to better grip the line, but even so their hands are cut and deeply scarred. When a big fish takes the bait, it is a pure test of strength, with no finesse about it.

A foreign angler with his fortune in fine equipment and his

Piroguemen outbound, Soumbedioune

Home with the catch

dreams of a mention in the record book might call that a waste of a sporting fish. Still, it is pretty wonderful to see a pair of men together in a small boat, nearly out of sight of land in a sea suddenly blown up and cresting in six-foot waves—both of them *standing* sure-footed in the canoe as it heaves and pitches, gaining line with every powerful sweep of arm and shoulder, each of them trying to subdue a violent sword-billed creature more than half his own weight.

If African fishermen take their canoes out there, why couldn't a sportsman go along, but with his rod and reel, and meet the *espadon* on something like fairer and more equal terms? The answer is, he can. And some regularly do.

All along the shore of the *Cap Vert* peninsula and on up the coast toward Mauritania are sandy coves and inlets, and in nearly every one of those is a settlement of fisher folk. Locating a pirogueman is easy enough. The trick, unless you happen to be fluent in the Wolof tongue, is to find one who speaks French. And then to bargain a price.

The discussion is not to be undertaken in haste. When finally settled on, the sum will be reasonable—a fraction of the cost of a commercial charter. But it must be arrived at deliberately, with no room left for misunderstanding. Senegalese fishermen are, in the main, hearty and fair-minded fellows. But like men of the sea anywhere, they also can be rough-natured and stubbornly independent. An African fishing village, with everyone tired from a day in the sun and evening coming on, would be no place to get into an argument about money.

This day the sea stays gentle, the canoe plunging nimbly through the smooth swells, a huge pod of porpoises in genial convoy beneath and beside.

"Espadon," Ouzin cries suddenly, and in the same instant turns the pirogue. He has spied a sailfish feeding on the surface, its sail extended, and marks the place now, although the fish has disappeared. The baits skip over the waves behind. The

boatman kneels on the stern seat for a better angle of view. *"Il est la!"* he calls out. *It's there!*

The blue surface bulges and parts, and the fish comes sword and head and shoulders clear of the water to strike the bait. For an instant there is nothing more. Then the line begins going slowly out—then faster. The fisherman engages the reel brake and strikes upward with the rod. And stung by the hook, the fish goes directly away at racehorse speed—50 yards, 100 yards, more, all in one blinding rush—and at the end of that comes straight up and out in a furious, acrobatic leap, big as a log against the sky.

And that is just the beginning. It will be another 40 minutes before the issue is decided and the fish is in the boat.

You only have to watch it done once to understand perfectly why some men put the pursuit of the *espadon* ahead of career and family. *Understand* it, that is—even if not necessarily always to condone.

31

A STORM OF DRUMMING has begun to gather. And not all of it is for rain, though certainly some is.

At Soumbedioune village just north along the seafront a ceremony with drums and dancing was held last week. Men dressed up in women's clothes and women in men's, and the hope of this comical affair, a Senegalese explained, was to amuse the gods and perhaps cause them to laugh until they wept a rain or two. Alas, the sky remained cloudless.

The government is of mixed mind about all this drumming. There is feeling in some quarters that the collective thunder of the tom-toms may actually *prevent* the rain from coming, and last year there was talk of putting a stop to it by decree. But then the wet season came early and lasted long, and the issue was shelved. Now, with the rains once more dangerously late and the fist of drought closing again on the Sahel, the debate may be revived.

Some of the current drumming, however, has nothing to do with the weather. An important Muslim holiday is approaching,

Bargaining the price of sheep

and because it is a time of gift-giving the merchants on the streets around the Sandaga market are competing feverishly for sales. Outside many of the open-fronted shops hired drummers are stationed, sometimes several at one store and dozens along a street. The merchants are betting that, whatever influence tom-toms may have on gods, they will bring business in. At every shop the rhythm of the drums is different. But together, they blend into a larger and oddly coherent rumble—pulsating, growing in volume through the afternoon, until by early evening the whole neighborhood of the market throbs with alarming energy.

Also on this coming feast day, tradition commands that each household of the faithful should slaughter a sheep. One of the supermarkets, as a promotion, has several of them on live display in an elevated cage, to be given away to lucky customers. Demand has driven up the price of sheep by multiples in a fortnight, although thousands of them can be seen tied to trees or simply wandering loose in the city, stepping out in front of cars with utter indifference to their sudden value.

Bad as the holiday is for sheep, it is even worse for public order. In a poor country—and especially in the capital, where so many marginal people are daily witnesses to the indulgence of power but are excluded from any of its spoils—this gathering atmosphere of celebration and gift-giving and sheep-killing seems to bring with it a mood of urgency and bitter resentment.

Street hustlers bear down upon their targets, especially Europeans and obvious tourists, with greater determination, and can get ill-tempered when refused or ignored. Reports of house burglaries are on the rise. And one hears with disturbing frequency, now, of purse-snatchings and even physical assaults by thieves in full light of day.

It is a case of custom requiring what the means of many cannot supply. The authorities seem not much concerned by this unpleasantness, for police rarely are in evidence in the locations of the worst predations. Their efforts appear to be concentrated on halting drivers along roads into and out of the city, in the hope of catching one whose papers are not quite in order and perhaps extracting a bribe. Policemen, too, have to give gifts and slaughter sheep.

After the holiday, people here say, the desperation passes and the poverty, though no less punishing, is borne with more resignation. For now, one arranges one's day around the temper of the town, going out less at night and not, if one can help it, on foot; staying off the corniche at lonely hours; avoiding certain streets and shunning especially the Place de l'Indépendance; taking care to make one's visits to the crowded market area in the morning or early afternoon, before the rumble of drums pounding through the heat has driven spirits to too florid a pitch.

Moussa, the day guard, is away now on a month's annual leave. But in this time it is the nights that are of main concern. And the night guard, Thiam, is exactly the kind of man one is glad to have at the gate.

He is a husky, thick-shouldered man with a gravelly bass voice and a smile so quick and friendly that just to see him is a happy event. He has five words of English: *How are you?* and *I'm fine.* Thiam is a boxer in the 175-pound class, though it would take some hard training to trim him back down to that. When he goes into his fighter's shuffle, filling the air with heavy hooks and uppercuts, you are glad it's just for fun. Of sixty-seven matches, he has lost only ten, all of them on points. No man has ever knocked him out.

He may have another fight this month, and if so, Thiam says, he would be glad if the people of the house cared to attend. They wouldn't dream of missing it. Meantime, they sleep like babies in his care.

32

𝒞HE CRIPPLED BOY'S STATION is on a street corner where larger, abler fellows sell bananas and mangoes to people whose cars stop for the traffic light. The vendors are aggressive, working quickly down the line, thrusting their merchandise through the open car windows and haggling over price. The crippled boy has nothing to offer but his smile, and at first you do not even notice that.

You see only his terrible deformity—legs withered to lifeless leather straps that are permanently contorted, maybe even *knotted,* below and behind him. They must be without sensation, because they are gray with dust and scuffed from having been dragged through the gravel of the roadside. You see that, and you look away quickly and pretend a sudden intense interest in the bananas one of the vendors is shoving through the car window. Then the traffic signal changes and you drive on with huge relief.

That's how it is the first time, the fifth, the tenth. There are beggars everywhere. How can you look at them all?

But that corner is on the way to several necessary places. You have to pass there often. And one day, without meaning to, you notice how clean the boy keeps himself, except of course for his hands, on which he walks, and the part of him that drags behind. His short-sleeved shirt is always freshly laundered, crisply pressed. It must mean that someone cares for him. He is not just some human wreck discarded there on the corner. He has a life.

The next time, or the time after, you find the courage to look at his face. And there is the amazement. It is a face filled with absolute, uncontainable joy. The eyes sparkle with humor and recognition. He knows the people in all the cars that regularly pass his corner. What else has he to do except remember the people, whether they look at him or not?

But it's his smile that takes the breath. It is not a smile of pleading or ingratiation. There is no self-pity in it, or pretense of bravery. *It just explodes across his face*—a spontaneous eruption of his unreasonable happiness at simply being. It mocks misfortune, that smile. It mocks and shames the glumness of anyone, anywhere, who ever whined or was embittered by bad luck. It celebrates life with the same force and virtuosity you feel when you see or hear a gifted athlete or musician perform, or watch Baryshnikov suspended weightless in a flying leap.

Sometimes a coin will be passed to him from the window of a car. Sometimes the light remains green and the traffic flows on uninterrupted. No difference. His happiness is the same either way.

You find yourself not dreading that corner any more.

Then you notice yourself going that way deliberately.

Then you are disappointed if you pass and, for some reason, he is not there. The coin is ready in your hand, and you feel cheated not to be able to give it—not as charity, but in gratitude.

Finally, you forget that he is crippled at all, just as he seems to have forgotten. The power of his happiness has made the useless parts of him disappear. And you think of him only as the boy with the wonderful smile.

33

𝒯HE CAR IS POINTED ALONG THE ROAD to the airport, and from the back seat she is singing them a lonely-heartbreak song. It is midnight, so the road is nearly empty. She finishes that song and sings another one she wrote herself, in calypso rhythm, whose lyrics tell about the time she stripped naked and danced on a nightclub table in Monrovia, Liberia.

"That's great," they all say when she stops singing. "That's wonderful."

"You like it?"

"It's great!" they tell her. The others in the car are praying earnestly that they can somehow get her on the plane. At the moment she is under control, but they have seen how quickly she can change.

She is telling them about how she married an old man in Liberia who was rich as anything, part of the upper crust. But then she got confused about a lot of things and flew home to her momma to get her mind straight. And then Sergeant Doe and his gang took over the government and all the ones she knew were out, so she never went back.

"Dumbest thing I ever did," she says. They don't know whether she means that running out on him was the dumbest thing, or marrying him in the first place. "Anyway, he's dead now. But I heard from his son I'm going to inherit some of his land. In about December, I think it is. Will you tell me what the hell I'm gonna do with eight acres in Liberia?" They couldn't. "Maybe I'll build a house on it, grow bananas."

Meantime, she said, her dog had died at Kennedy Airport in New York after being shut up too long in a stuffy crate. She'd taken him out of the crate and he'd died in her arms. And crooked agents and promoters had cheated her out of $70,000 for concerts in the last six months.

If you are old enough to have been listening to pop records in the 1950s and early '60s, probably you would recognize her name. And if you heard it now, or heard one of those golden oldies, you might wonder what ever became of her.

Well, what became of her lately is that she came to Africa with a tour—not a singing tour, just a *tourist* tour, on which Dakar was the last stop. Then, for reasons unknown to anyone else and not even very clear to her now, when her tour group went home to the States she didn't go with it, so her return plane ticket was no good. That was a week or more ago. She was staying at the Novotel, and the money she had left was melting away fast. Then she got in an argument with the people at the hotel, and when they didn't know who she was or that she was famous she pulled a knife on them, which did not endear her to the management.

This is the second time in two nights she has been driven to the airport. The night before, she had acted crazy and made a scene, refusing to get on the plane. The Air Afrique people had said fine, that was terrific, because they didn't want her on *their* plane anyway. So she went back to the hotel, and the people who had gotten themselves in the unenviable position of looking after her had called a doctor, who didn't think she was drunk or on drugs, just mentally disturbed and sad—someone who didn't understand why fame had not lasted as long as she wished it had, and who had gotten herself in a crack about money and probably was a little scared.

They figured that one of two things would happen. Either she would pull her knife again and maybe hurt somebody, or she would run out of money and not be able to pay her bill. Then the police would get involved. They had some idea about the inside of an African jail, even if she didn't. So they had come for her again tonight to make another try at the airport—the 2:45 in the morning Sunday flight to New York.

She was eating dinner in the hotel restaurant, taking her time about it. Finally she came out, wearing a black skirt and a glittery gold lamé blouse with the zipper stuck exactly in the middle so it was open both above and below the stuck place.

Her bags already were down in the lobby. One of the people got some francs from her to settle her night's bill. The checkout clerk did a foolish thing. He tried to charge twice for her supper, perhaps hoping to pocket the second payment. They demanded to see the paper, and the meal clearly was paid. "Listen here," one of them told the clerk, when she stepped away a moment to check about her suitcase. "You make a problem and we wash our hands of it. She's yours." The clerk stamped the bill *Paid* and they started out to the car, where she got in a screaming argument on the hotel drive with some woman none of the others had ever seen. Then they got her actually *in* the car and she was talking and singing to them as they drove, seeming pretty much under control although they knew it was a minute-to-minute thing.

Now, finally, they are in the parking lot outside the airport terminal, getting her things out of the back of the car. "Zip my back, will you?" she tells one of them. But it is firmly stuck, with the zipper separated above and below. The glittery gold blouse is too tight for her, and he couldn't have zipped it anyway under the best of circumstances. Even after midnight the air is hot. Sweat keeps running down into his eyes, and he is thinking, *Holy Christ, I won't be able to get it shut and she'll go clear off her rocker and that will be the end of the plane for tonight.*

Then she forgets about the zipper, goes in the terminal and up the steps to the lounge, flops in a chair and orders a Flag beer. "Okay," she says, "go over it again now. Who's going to meet me?"

They tell who will meet her in Washington, D.C. After about a dozen trans-Atlantic phone calls they finally have found someone who will do that as a favor.

"Yeah," she says, her eyes suddenly hard and suspicious. "That's Washington. What about New York?"

They tell her the airline passenger agent will meet her at Kennedy and help her through customs and be sure she gets to her Washington flight.

"Don't give me no *agent* crap!" she screams at them. "You think I want to die? Name. What's his name? I wanta *name!*"

They don't have a name. One of them says he will do what he can, and goes down to the ticket counter to see if he can get the airline to send a Telex to New York. She is getting a lot of service, but by now everyone's fear that she will not get on the airplane is very large.

She is telling again about how her dog died in her arms at Kennedy Airport. "That goddamn place has got blood on it," she says. "I'm afraid of it. If everything doesn't go exactly right when I get there I'm going to die." She begins to cry.

The one who went to send the Telex comes back.

"We still don't have a name," he says. But he shows her the printed copy of the message. It says that she is a very distinguished person, a famous singer, and that she must naturally receive extra special consideration and assistance immediately upon landing in New York. It's a brilliant piece of writing under extreme pressure, and seems to cheer her up.

"So you'll be met at the plane," says the one who sent it.

"That's right," the others tell her. "When the plane lands, just tell them you aren't moving anywhere until you see an agent."

She has forgotten about wanting a name.

"You know, I hate to leave," she tells them. "This is a beautiful place. These are beautiful people. Except they don't know crap about how to run a hotel. They've got a beautiful suite on the top floor that I didn't find out about until today. That's where I ought to be. I could sell my furniture in California and come live in that suite and show them how to make some money. The manager is a nice man. I think I can work something out."

They all nod seriously without saying anything. They look at their watches and see it is after 2 a.m.

"I want some of the action here," she tells them. "I want a piece of that hotel." Then she begins to cry again. "Aw, who the hell wants any goddamn hotel?" she says through her tears. "What I want is a piece of a *bank*."

The loudspeaker announces the flight to New York.

"You know," she tells them, "I didn't really think I was going to go. I better get rid of these." She opens her purse and gives them two knives, a large pair of scissors and a long, silver dagger-type letter opener. Then she closes her purse and they walk with her to the departure gate.

"Keep those for me," she says. "I'm just going home to get a few things straightened out. It wouldn't surprise me if I'm back in a couple of weeks."

She goes through the gate, through passport control, then straight *past* the metal detector and on out of sight. The others hurry back up to the lounge, where they can watch through the window. One of them already has alerted the chief steward on the flight that she is a nervous lady who should not be given too much to drink and should be encouraged to take the pills the doctor prescribed to keep her calm.

The passengers go out in bunches through the heat across the dark taxiway toward the plane. From the lounge window, she can readily be distinguished by the gold blouse that spans in a double V above and below the stuck zipper. The passengers all climb the metal stair. The tarmac is empty. But the people watching from the window do not feel absolutely, totally safe until the plane door closes and the portable steps are rolled away. Then, giddy with relief, they go out to the car and back toward the city.

"The things you get involved in," one of them says. They are glad to be rid of her, and at the same time cannot help wondering what will become of her at the other end. One thing they do know: Africa is no place to come to find yourself when you are holding your life together by a thread.

34

FOR MILE AFTER MILE as one travels the highway northward from Dakar, as far as the eye can see to either side, the landscape is the same. No, not *quite* the same. By gradual degrees, the country actually worsens.

At first there are scrubby thickets of acacia, occasional dusty bushes and clumps of dead grass, some sort of fibrous creeping vine and once in a great while, along the shallow groove of a dry streambed, a furtive hint of green. Beside one thatched village, a bore hole and pivot sprinkler have even turned a whole small hillside lush with plots of leafy vegetables.

Farther on, though, these slight encouragements disappear entirely, and there are only the trees, spaced well apart, some dead and barkless, the others increasingly stunted and gnarled by thirst. The bare earth pales into something close to pure sand—then *is* sand, pushed up in rippled windrows and spilling out of the emptiness to half cover the road. Yet even here, as in the whole of the journey, not a kilometer passes without disclosing some spectacle of diligence and pain.

In the heat shimmer, a line of women can be seen with huge clay jars balanced on their heads, trudging tiredly on their lives' unending circuit between hut and distant water well. Walking at roadside are men in family groups and larger gangs, each with a long-handled hoe, all going somewhere to spend another day in what they imagine to be a field. On a little rise, in dark outline, are two peasants and a burro. The burro pulls an iron-wheeled, single-bladed plow. One man steers the plow, the other pulls the burro. The plow stirs lifeless sand.

These scenes, repeated several hundred times, cease to be starkly picturesque and become, instead, first depressing and finally, in an irrational kind of way, utterly senseless and even *infuriating*.

One is gripped, for just an instant, by the crazy urge to leap from the car and run out onto the scalding roadside, screaming to all those pitiful toilers: *It's no use! Give it up! Nothing will come of it, though it's not your fault. There are just places on Earth where human beings were not meant to live!*

One doesn't do that, of course—only in the mind, silently, behind the closed window of the air-conditioned car. Then the sad tableau of people and beasts and sand slips behind, and the road tops the next rise to reveal another exactly like it.

This is the peanut-growing region of northwestern Senegal. And since the nation depends on peanuts as its one large cash export, what happens here is of enormous human and political importance. If the rains do not come soon, the peanut crop will fail and the country will sink even deeper into penury. The peasants will then replant the sand with their subsistence crop, millet. And if the rains still do not come, the millet, too, will fail. And the people will starve.

So they are doing the only thing they know to do. And while the region may, indeed, be inhospitable to life, it is not entirely true to say that they are bound to it by ignorance or their inability to imagine another, better way to live. The cultivable

150

Fishermen's graves with nets, Saint-Louis

Senegal River at Saint-Louis

lands of Senegal are limited by deserts to the north and east. With the dry years following one after the last, the land is ruined and the deserts are advancing. One day the howling waste may be here. Meantime, there is nothing to do except put in seed and pray. Because the cities, too, are failed and desperate places. There is no more or better land to be had. There is no place else to go.

After four hours of looking at this desolation, the travelers arrive at last at the Senegal River, on the country's northern frontier. Large irrigation dams have been flung across the river, in hope of impounding its flow for distribution to the agricultural north. Maybe it will work. It *has* to work, the Senegalese know, or it is only a matter of time until the Sahara claims it all.

Saint-Louis itself is a genteel ruin, rather as the French Quarter of New Orleans might look after being reduced by twenty-five years of hard times and neglect to a state of advanced decrepitude. During early colonial times, this town at the river's mouth was the base from which France ruled all its West African holdings and was a lively, stylish and reasonably prosperous place. But reverses came one upon the other. First the colonial administration was moved in 1902 to Dakar, leaving Saint-Louis as the capital only of the Senegal territory. And at the country's independence in 1960, Dakar became seat of the national government as well.

Wealth, influence and style all left in a rush, and Saint-Louis today has the wistful air of a near ghost town, where the French proprietors of the *Hôtel La Résidence* seemed touchingly glad for visitors. That's where the Americans stopped the night. The others in the car had the duty of continuing on business several more hours up the coast to Nouakchott, the capital of Mauritania—a piece of true desert ruled by a junta calling itself the Military Committe for National Salvation, though salvation almost certainly is out of reach.

Nouakchott is a mud town on the seashore, a capital so

unimposing that a foreign naval officer bound for the place once missed it entirely, ran his ship aground and was relieved of his command. On returning from there the next day, the travelers bring reports of a primitive, cheerless city full of fanatical and unfriendly Moors, a place so uninviting that even drought-smitten northern Senegal is, by comparison, a garden. In their opinion, whatever the damage to his naval career, the captain of that errant ship was better off in the end for having missed Nouakchott.

35

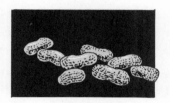

CREDIT IT TO THE DRUMS and the dancers. Or to the interventions of the holy men with a merciful Allah. Or to the simple entreaties of the humble country folk, prostrate on their prayer mats under the devouring sun. Or to plain luck, of which there has been precious little in recent times.

Give the credit to anyone or anything. There's enough to go around. Because it finally has rained again—and not just an hour's tantalizing downpour like the two rains before. This one came businesslike and steady for part of a day and all that night and most of the next day.

The storm began at Saint-Louis in the far north, from where the travelers were coming back by car, and moved with and ahead of them the whole way down to Dakar. Across all that reach of the country, people took to their fields in great numbers—some following behind burros or horses (for sand turns obligingly to the plowshare in any weather) and others just standing like statues in the deluge, faces raised to it, grateful to be gloriously wet.

Water pooled on the highway. Every ditch became a swollen freshet, every slight depression a lake, for such was this rain that even the driest land could not drink it quickly enough. What normally is a four-hour journey took nearly six. And no one complained. No one would have dared.

It may strike a reader that these accounts have spoken excessively, tediously, about the weather. But that is the nature of life and of daily conversation in this part of the world, where no other subject—not wars or threats of war, not even the fate of government itself—can begin to generate the urgency of interest in the question of rain, or the lack of it.

For example, an agronomist recently fixed a date on which, if the general rains had not arrived by then, the peanut crop would be finished. And what does the peanut mean to Senegal? Only "everything." Some sense of the fragility of this economy and its paucity of foreign trade may come from knowing that Senegal's largest export to the United States is, of all things, tropical birds, and that its principal U.S. import, apart from aid-related food shipments, is secondhand clothing. It is the peanut crop, most of it sold through the government monopoly to oil producers in France, that in effect finances the country.

The fatal day for the peanuts, in the agronomist's calculation, fell on a Friday. This great rain came at the beginning of that week.

All through the night the storm beat against the window shutters and water gushed noisily from the eaves. In the morning it continued undiminished. Cars traveled the city with their headlights on. But people did not stay indoors. They went about their errands, water pelting and streaming from them, with not a sign of inconvenience. The sense of elation and relief seemed almost palpable in the air, as in a country that had just received news of an armistice.

"The Sahel Is Watered!" rejoiced the banner headline in the next edition of *Le Soleil*, the national daily.

So, for the moment, the peanut is saved. The crop will sprout and grow. Whether it will mature, bear fruit and ripen to a harvest is yet another matter. More rains will have to come—rains that, with the lateness of the season, are by no means sure.

And even after that there is a new hazard: Locusts. They rise and fly sometimes in clicking clouds of millions, darkening the sun and consuming everything green in their path. The people whose business is bugs say that conditions this year are right to bring a plague of them. So, with the rain watch over, a locust alert has gone out to diplomatic missions all across the Sahel. Maybe they will not come. Or, if they do come, maybe they can somehow be halted.

In Africa, it seems, survival always requires just one more miracle.

36

IN 1963 A LITTLE GROUP of Benedictine monks arrived from France to found a monastery at a place called Keur Moussa, an hour east and north of Dakar, and sing their devotions to an accompaniment of African instruments—the drum and the balafon and the kora, a twenty-one-string harp.

The independence of Senegal still was new then, but the piece of land they settled, like all around it, already was far gone in exhaustion. Decades, generations, of uninterrupted peanut cultivation had sapped the ground of its slight fertility. With the advent of the railroad, the last of the forest had been cut to fuel the fire boxes of the locomotives. The ruin of the fragile ecosystem was complete, and the sandy terrain lay fully exposed to the cruelty of erratic moisture and desiccating heat.

The monks set out to reclaim the broken land, although residents of the area found their efforts amusing and promised that they would fail. First they drilled for, and found, water. That was their only luck, or possibly a gift of Providence. All the rest they did by the work of their hands.

They planted rows of cashew trees whose thick foliage would deflect the scouring winds that for much of the year blow down from the northeast out of the furnace of the Sahara. Then, in the areas sheltered by the cashews, they set out orchards of mangoes, grapefruit, papayas and coco palms. To nourish their trees they contrived a system of drip irrigation on the Israeli model—a network of slender perforated hoses through which water is fed slowly into the ground around the outer root zone, reducing the waste of evaporation.

Slowly, a hectare (2.47 acres) at a time, they expanded their domain of growing things. With so much patience have they proceeded that, even now, of the monastery's hundred hectares only about fifteen are under cultivation. But how utterly astonishing the transformation has been—and how productive. Led this day by Brother Louis-Marie along the paths of that vast garden, one sees at every turn such exploding fruitfulness that it is possible to believe, against all the other evidence, that Africa may once have been Eden after all.

Brother Louis-Marie is Senegalese, one of the only twenty French and African confreres in the small monastic community. He is a slight, handsome man, serene and soft-spoken, and his pleasure in what has been achieved is evident.

The limber branches of the mango trees bend all the way to ground under the weight of their incredible bearing. The limbs of the grapefruit, too, are heavy with a large crop contracted for sale even before it has ripened. Enclosed by a border of long-needled pines is a considerable plantation of bananas, and other orderly plots yield melons, green vegetables and potatoes by the hundredweight for the brothers' use. In one corner of the grounds, a wire fence surrounds a neat village of thatched huts—pretty little houses, lived in not by people but by hundreds of rabbits raised for the table and for market.

Not one square meter is wasted. Where the earth is not cultivated it is carpeted entirely with dark grass. Beside and between things grown for practical use are others planted for their flower or fragrance, and for the harvest of pleasure they give. Everywhere there is a flash of colored birds among the leaves, the music of their songs; everywhere a sense of shade and surprising coolness. In this remarkable place, the ground underfoot breathes fecundity and promise. And the astonishing truth is that all of this—every bit of it—was undertaken during exactly the same years when the Sahel of Africa was being savaged by one of the worst extended droughts in the whole of recorded history.

Where the monks' labors end, there stretches away in every direction still a heartbreak of ruined land, a terrain so empty and sterile as to appear beyond hope of reclamation. And, indeed, so hostile is it to life that even the serpents have fled it and come in to Eden—wicked serpents, some of them, green mambas and cobras that slide silently through the greenness and dappled shade of the garden of Keur Moussa.

What is one to make of this place? What outrageous speculations does it provoke? Dare one even toy with the notion that, given time enough and care enough, great areas of the ruined country might fruit in much this same way?

"The mountain cannot be moved in a day," says Brother Louis-Marie. "Large projects do not succeed. Each year, each day, you must move only a small piece of the mountain. You develop that small area, and when you have finished you can go on to the next." The mountain to be moved in Senegal alone is great—the mountain of all of Africa incomparably vaster still. He passes his eyes from the one lonely island of greenery to the enormity of those barrens that lie beyond.

"Persevere," he says. The word is like a hopeful whisper down an unimaginable corridor of time. "One has to *persevere*."

Brother Louis-Marie at Keur Moussa

37

IN THE PRESS ALMOST DAILY CAN BE found mention of the goings and comings around the continent of African chiefs of state who, taken as a group, are a much-traveled lot. These peregrinations are not without certain hazard, as more than one president has come home from a triumph of statesmanship to find a general sitting in his chair—or, if he himself already was a general, to find a sergeant or a flight lieutenant sitting there.

But the lure of travel must be irresistible, because leaders still run the risk.

A good deal of pomp attends these visits. For pure ceremony, of course, no one has yet touched the once-and-only emperor of the Central African Republic, Jean-Bedel Bokassa, a demented gnome who received pleasure from beating his subjects to death with his own hands and who emptied his country's treasury to finance his self-coronation.

Even here in Senegal, a place of relative restraint, the fanfare is considerable. The prime minister of Great Britain may slip into Washington for a conversation with the American president and be gone again practically unnoticed. But such modesty does not become the leaders of frailer republics. The arrival of a state visitor is an event generally involving the scarlet-robed palace guard, copious Mercedes-Benzes, platoons of uniformed outriders on motorcycles with sirens howling. And, when politically advantageous, manufactured crowds.

Never mind that some of these visitors may not even have countries to represent.

The other day, on a road outside Dakar, traffic was ordered to the shoulder and halted while one of these processions swept grandly past. The line of black limousines all rushing at high speed toward the city along a highway swept clean of lesser travelers gave to the moment a sense of breathless importance.

"Yasser Arafat," the driver, Ibrahima, said, not seeming too impressed.

There was no way of knowing for sure if it was the PLO leader, or, if so, which car he was riding in, since all the faces were hidden behind dark-tinted glass. But it was a fact that the previous day's paper, *Le Soleil,* had reported he was coming for talks with the Senegalese president.

What use might be expected to come from discussions between the leader of one of the world's poorest countries and the leader of one of the world's most disreputable revolutions is best left to history's judgment. What any of it had to do with the profound needs of the Senegalese people is an even greater mystery.

The best rumor is that Arafat came here to borrow a razor.

38

SOMETIMES THE HARDNESS OF LIFE is quite forgotten. The wretched poverty, the disfigurement and venality and rage and the relentless clutter, all pass from mind. In their place comes a sense of almost inexpressible sweetness. And you realize, with a little start of wonder, that your heart is strangely at peace here.

It can happen even in the city, early on a weekend morning with the air still cool and shadows darkly pooled, with birds chirping their waking songs and the smell of new loaves floating out from bakers' doorways and the few people abroad at that hour seen passing distantly along the tree-tunnel of the street.

The likeliest time, though, is when you are driving back from somewhere on a country road at the end of afternoon, and the fire goes off the land and the light softens.

The last shepherds can be seen coming with their flocks, each flock bunched close to make a single dark creature with a hundred legs, the herders tall behind. At a pool of a roadside stream, a woman bends to wash her hair—woman and trees and orange clouds reflected in the mirror of the water, like a painting by an African Renoir.

The long march of another day is finished. People are one day nearer their destinations, whatever those destinations may be, however proximate or far. And now, in the suspended moment before night and sleeping, they relish the gift of a little ease. Women talk together at the village well. Men with hands calloused by the hoe squat on their heels in the universal country way, their backs against woven-reed fences, speaking of the weather, calculating how many showers will yet be needed to make a crop. The huts, their grass roofs bound in decorative topknots, become momentarily golden in the soft light, then merge all together into one long silhouette, the line of the roofs interrupted by the minaret of a mud-brick mosque.

Inside the lighted doorway of a little Arab store stand young men wearing T-shirts printed with legends they cannot read—shirts that arrived in that place, along with Bob Marley tapes and miniature cassette players, by some miracle or unaccountable accident of commerce. *It Takes a Stud To Build a House,* reads one shirt. *I Love Fig Newtons,* says another.

Market women with their skirts gathered all about them sit cross-legged behind roadside piles of nuts, melons and mangoes. Men wait with coconuts to sell, or hold up two-foot-long gray ocean fish to be viewed as possible suppers by riders in the passing cars. Horse-cart taxis, slow and reflectorless, claim a full lane of the road. On a bench, a girl braids another's hair. Farther on, people have gathered in a circle around three drummers playing. The *crème* of the village—tall women in pastel gowns, and taller men in stately white ones, their carriage announcing privilege—walk slowly, to be seen.

All of this gradually darkens, darkens in the failing light, the way a melody fades and sweetens on its way toward being silence. Then there are no more figures. Just shadows before a light, the suggestions of movement somewhere near. Then not even those. Only the sightless dark, and the beams of the headlights lancing through it, and the belief that you have been allowed a brief insight into lives of tenderness and repose.

That is perfectly fatuous, of course. The realities have in no way changed, and the realities of life in such a place are disease and futility, bondage of one sort or other, premature aging, early death. It is just that, for a sentimental moment, you have imagined you saw beyond those to something else and better: To Africa as it once was, perhaps; or might have been; or as it meant to be.

Probably it is wrong to give in, that way, to romantic foolishness. Part of the process of becoming acclimated here is to learn not to notice many of the hardest and most painful truths. And that should be resisted, because there are some things one should never allow oneself to get used to. In any case, the feeling does not come often. And it does not last long.

39

FOR SHEEP IN SENEGAL, after a halcyon spell of indulgence and special pampering, this past weekend was the time of the long knives.

Just after daylight on Saturday, at the club where foreigners sometimes meet to play tennis in the cool of morning, there was heard from behind the high wall of the adjoining house a sudden bleat of surprise as one of the sacrificial creatures felt the blade at its throat. It seemed to take a long time for that first cry to gurgle away to silence, and for many minutes the players' thoughts were not entirely on their game.

Later the same morning, two more sheep were dispatched by the residents of the compound in back of the museum across the street, and the pair of bloody heads, fixedly staring, were set out on the sidewalk while inside the compound men pulled off the skins and readied the meat for the fire.

Across the whole of the land, the ceremony—gentle touch of hand, the glint of sharpened steel, a death rattle—was endlessly repeated, for custom commands that on this Islamic holiday every pious family should slaughter a *mouton* and give a feast. The obligation is considered binding by all who can possibly afford it, and even many who cannot.

The holiday's exact timing is not fixed by standard date, as on a Western calendar, but rather is determined at the last minute according to the sightings of the moon by a leading *marabout,* or holy man. In Senegal, the matter is complicated by the divided allegiance of the country's Muslims—who are four-fifths of the population—between several Islamic brotherhoods.

Rivalry among the principal brotherhoods, while no longer fierce or militant, is nonetheless real. And it extends even to such seemingly minor things as the setting of holy days. The religious leaders, jealous of their prerogatives, rarely manage to sight the moon at the same time or in quite the same way, with the result that some Senegalese celebrate on one day and the others a day or two later. It is as if Americans, depending on whether they were Baptists or Presbyterians, observed two Christmases and two Easters.

As late as Thursday afternoon, the rulings on the state of the moon still were unknown and there was an air of general suspense. Would the holidays by chance coincide? Or would they, as many hoped, be declared on Friday and Monday, prolonging to four days the period of national rest? As it turned out—and not everyone was happy about it—they fell on successive days of the weekend.

So the sheep killing by part of the people on Saturday was repeated by the rest of them on the following morning. And to compound the confusion of this attractively tolerant and unfanatical place, the doomed bleats of the Sunday sheep and the cries of the muezzin rose to mingle with the chiming bells of the Roman Catholic cathedral, summoning to early mass the minority of an altogether different faith with no sanguinary duties to perform.

Bocar, the cook, took off early one afternoon last week to buy his *mouton*. The next day he reported that, though it had taken him six hours and much hard bargaining, he finally had gotten a good one for 24,000 Senegalese francs, something less than half a month's pay. He counted himself lucky. Some people he knew had given 40,000 francs. And the very wealthy, for whom the price of their sheep is a badge of conspicuous consumption, occasionally boast of having paid the equivalent of $600 and more for one fat animal.

Now, he is a good Muslim, Bocar. He also has six children to raise on a cook's wage. Moreover, he knows that livestock traders are clever men, and he is overtaken sometimes by the unworthy suspicion that, at certain seasons, more than the simple law of supply and demand may be at work in determining the worth of a *mouton*.

In choosing the day to celebrate, however, he has discretion. A Malian by origin, he owes his loyalty to none of the main brotherhoods here. So as regards the moon, if not the price of sheep, Bocar is his own man.

40

ONE QUAILS AT THE ATTEMPT to compress into a few brief lines a subject to which serious scholars have devoted whole learned books. But at least a sketchy understanding of Islam's curious permutations here in Senegal is essential to knowing how the society is organized and how power flows, so the effort has to be made.

In the centuries before Europe turned its colonizing eye on Africa, say the historians, this was far from being a tranquil and idyllic place. Indigenous warlords and their armies surged across the stage, fighting their bitter, unrecorded wars. A succession of kingdoms and empires—often brutal, some quite magnificent—flowered and waned.

Colonial penetration and eventual subjugation broke the power of the traditional chiefs, who became little more than petty administrators bound to execute the orders of the French or else be summarily replaced. Thus was created a vacuum of credible leadership, which the missionaries of Islam, sweeping south and west like a wind across the desert, were quick to fill.

But what evolved here was Islam with a difference.

At various times and places in Senegal during the last two hundred years, certain Muslim teachers and holy men, proclaiming themselves—or proclaimed by others—to be divine interpreters of the Prophet's word, gathered around them groups of disciples and, diverging from the mainstream of the faith, became, in effect, the leaders of subdenominations of their own. In the colonial era, they rallied intellectual resistance to the threat of total cultural conquest.

These brotherhoods, as they came to be called, or *confréries*, sometimes mystical in character and sometimes eminently practical, all are organized along the same general lines. At the top is the principal leader, descended by blood relation from the original founder or one of his intimates, surrounded by a coterie—a kind of religious court—of men similarly well born.

From that center, power runs outward in an elaborate hereditary network of descending importance, from the Khalif General to, say, the chief *marabout* of a city like Dakar, to his subordinate in some dusty, mud-walled provincial village. The exact definition of *marabout* is elusive. Strictly speaking, it refers to a religious teacher. In practice, he is likely also to be part politician, part businessman and fund-raiser, intermediary between the faithful and their God (a role not acknowledged by classical Islam), a giver of blessings, diviner of the future and, when called upon, worker of magic and dispeller of charms.

It is easy to find humor in things we do not understand, and of all the features of Senegalese life the role of the brotherhoods may, to a Westerner, be the least understandable. Suffice that they filled a need for social structure that resulted from the destruction of the traditional chiefdoms. In the view of many who know the country well, the unifying influence of Islam helped to transcend regional and ethnic factionalism and thus deserves part of the credit for sparing Senegal the fragmentation experienced in other parts of post-independence Africa.

171

All but a fraction of Senegal's Muslims give allegiance to one of the three principal *confréries*, of which the Qadiri brotherhood is the oldest, the Tijani brotherhood the largest in numbers and the Mouride brotherhood the youngest, the richest and the most powerful. And what does this allegiance imply?

It means, if the disciple is employed, that he will give some part of his earnings to the work of the brotherhood. If, as in the case of a great many Mourides, he is a peasant farmer, it means that he will help till the *marabout's* vast estates—sometimes for as much as ten years without compensation—and also will tithe a portion of the harvest from his own small plot either to his local religious leader or directly to the Khalif.

In return, the *marabouts* hold out the promise of paradise in the life to come, give advice in important matters of their disciples' present lives and exert their sometimes considerable political influence to advance the interests of the brotherhood. In effect, money flows from the humble ranks upward, while authority is exercised from the top downward through the hierarchy of holy men. Whether the bargain is a fair one from the standpoint of the masses is a matter of individual judgment, and anyway is beside the point. It is how the society works.

The Mouride brotherhood was founded at the turn of this century by Amadu Bamba, whose reputation for scholarship and piety drew a growing circle of followers and caused the French, alarmed that his movement might turn against their interests, twice to exile him from the country. In fact, however, the Mourides were to be their most useful collaborators.

With the end of the slave trade, France had looked to the peanut in the hope of making the colony profitable. And the Mouride leadership, seizing the opportunity of changing times, focused their efforts among the poor and landless of the groundnut basin, establishing farming settlements, breaking out new lands for cultivation, preaching spiritual salvation through hard work in the fields of the *confrérie*. With the result that, by

The great mosque of Touba

the time of independence, the Mourides had put themselves in a position to virtually dominate production and distribution of the country's only real cash crop. Who controls the peanut, in a sense, controls Senegal.

The authority of the central government may be paramount in Dakar and a few other major cities, but the farther one travels from the center the more weakly its influence is felt. Whereas the power of the *marabouts* extends throughout the country, into commerce and politics and into the homes of the most illiterate villagers.

For Amadu Bamba's heirs, the seat of that power is the town of Touba, the holy city of Senegal's Mourides—holier, in the minds of many of them, than Mecca itself. It is reached by road two and one-half hours east from Dakar. One passes first through Thies, where the leftward branching highway bears north toward Saint-Louis. Straight on the road leads, through an ever more impoverished and depressing landscape whose brief mantle of green from the spotty rains cannot hide the thinness of the leached and sandy soil.

The next place of any size is Diourbel, a regional capital but a place of breathtaking hopelessness, in whose small, sad market mangoes and eggplants are sold not whole but in pieces and where vendors squat behind rags on which are laid out tragic little handfuls of shriveled peppers, puckered tomatoes and woody brown roots.

At Diourbel the road forks again, one branch bending south to Kaolack in the Sine Saloum, the other, which the travelers take, striking on to the northeast. Presently, on that route, one notices a change. The road looks to have been newly repaved and is immaculately kept. The peanut fields look greener, farther advanced and more promising than the ones before. Abruptly the pavement separates into four divided lanes, bordered by stately colonnades of trees in country where no trees ought by rights to be.

Then, still miles away, there appears exactly where the road diminishes to a point ahead a kind of vision. Cream-colored against the hazy blue of desert sky, the minarets of the great mosque of Touba vault above the table-flatness all around with a majesty to smite the imagination even of an unbeliever. The gifts of the rich, the pittances of the poor and the labor of the faithful built it. That is the approach to the heart of this force that is known as Mouridism.

41

WITHOUT ANY SUGGESTION OF A BREEZE, the sun bears down as mercilessly upon Touba as anywhere else in the scorched interior. And yet somehow—perhaps it is because of the uncommon abundance of leafy trees—this holy city, as midday nears, seems less smitten than simply serene.

The visitors' host is El Hadji Mouhamed Mahmoud Niang, the Khalif General's secretary for Arab affairs, a sort of foreign minister of the Mouride brotherhood. He is a princely man in a sweeping blue robe, tall and proud of bearing, his strikingly handsome black features utterly uncreased although the years have begun to frost his hair with white. His languages are Wolof and Arabic, so he speaks his greeting through an interpreter, a young relative of the Khalif who is home on holiday from the university. Then he leads across the great central square to a small building inside a compound where guests are received.

Persian carpets cover the floor, and couches are around the room with a low table in the center. Courtesies are exchanged, then a serving man appears with an ice chest full of bottled soft drinks. Within the limits of Touba, a town of 140,000 souls, there is not one hotel, not one restaurant. The laws of Islam are rigorously observed. No alcohol may be consumed, no drums played or folkloric spectacles performed, no lottery tickets sold, no tobacco or hemp smoked.

Mindful of this scarcity of services, the visitors have arrived in late morning, intending only a short visit. They have packed a lunch of sandwiches which they mean to eat somewhere on the road back. But now the serving man returns with a metal basin, a basket containing a bar of soap, a towel and a kettle of warm water which he pours over their hands as they wash. They are surprised and delighted by this hospitality. They think they are about to be served cookies, or perhaps some little cakes.

The serving man retires again, briefly. This time he returns with an enormous metal tray, which he puts on the table. Whatever is on the tray is draped entirely with a covering of white cloth. Then he whisks the cloth away. What is under it is an entire half-grown sheep, glazed golden-brown from slow cooking over an open fire. The Khalif's aides wish *bon appétit* and withdraw to let the visitors eat in privacy, leaving only the server to attend their possible wants.

Anyone who has never sat down to a whole sheep cooked like that—the skin crisp and curling, the meat suffused throughout with crushed pepper and other spices—deserves to know that it is worth doing. Beside the platter are loaves of bread warm from the oven. The visitors eat slowly, wordlessly, in true reverence, and they eat an indecent amount. They are thinking, *Ah, if only there were a little glass of wine to wash it down!* They have finished half the creature and are working on the other side when the serving man, possibly afraid they will injure themselves, takes the tray away and the host returns.

Would the guests like to go now to the grand mosque?

Touba mosque, interior

Of course they would. They find it to be a place of elegance and quiet, aromatic and wonderfully cool. In a sort of central court, Mouride pilgrims dip drinks of holy water from a marble pool. Avenues of marble columns lead off from there in splendid prospects of alternating light and shadow where men are seated in little groups on woven mats, discussing, and official calligraphers, books and papers spread around them, bend to their copying of the Prophet's words.

Might the visitors care to climb the minaret? Unfortunately, the elevator is out of order and they will have to take the spiral stair.

No matter, they'd like to do it. The Khalif's secretary draws from the folds of his robe a hand radio, into which he speaks a few soft words to someone. It's a long climb, he tells the guests, so he will wait below. Another, younger man accompanies them up. And, as promised, it's a taxing ascent, but the view from the highest turret, some two hundred fifty feet above the spreading plain, is sufficient reward.

Below, as in an aerial photograph, lies the town—orderly, functional, clean. If any clutter comes to the Khalif's eye, the escort explains, the saint has but to utter a word and all of Touba is made immaculate again. Across an open space can be seen the modern building that houses the brotherhood's library, directed by a professional librarian, its volumes, mostly in Arabic, indexed according to the Dewey decimal system. Nearer, in a separate chamber connected to the mosque, rest the remains of the brotherhood's founder, Amadu Bamba himself, in a tomb richly ornamented with gold. Beside it are displayed his artifacts: A battered trunk or two, some papers, his robe—the few poor earthly possessions of an ascetic.

From the great square, roads radiate out like spokes, running off without deviation across the undifferentiated landscape toward all the regions and principal towns of Senegal, reminding one that, for Mourides, Touba is the capital of the world. In so far as human labor can defeat this hostile climate, the desert has been made to bloom. For in the immediate environs of the town and some way beyond, a more fertile green cloaks the country. Beyond that, it starts to pale.

Looking down from there, strangely there comes to mind another garden spot, the grounds of the Benedictine monastery at Keur Moussa. The endeavors of the Mouride *confrérie* and of the Catholic monks, though vastly different in scale, are both miracles of accomplishment. And both are the product of faith—that commodity which governments in this part of the world seem least able to command. Could it be that faith, of one sort or other (perhaps any zealotry will do), is the means by which desperate societies might save themselves? The visitors can't pretend to know the answer, but the question lingers in their minds.

Descending the stairway, then, they are met by the surprising news that the Khalif himself will receive them in his residence. After passing through the gates of several walls, they are led finally into a sunny little parlor where the present ruler of all this religious empire waits.

Serigne Abdoul Ahad M'Backe is a man of 75 years upon whom the burden of sainthood weighs heavily. He wears a robe and turban, and the hairs of his arms shine like silver wires against his dark skin. His eyes behind plastic rimmed spectacles appear uncertain, or perhaps just tiredly amused. One suspects that people are very often led before him without his having the least notion of why they've come, or what they want, or what he is expected to say to them.

Under the woven-mat sun shelter in the courtyard outside his parlor, more people are waiting—will wait for days, if they must, to see him. The queue of supplicants never ends. And unlike these merely curious *toubabs*, the faithful bring him their gifts.

42

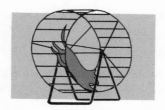

𝒯HE LADY SENATOR from the United States had planned to come to Senegal on Wednesday evening on a commercial flight from Ethiopia. But the plane in Addis Ababa was broken and couldn't fly, so she arrived instead at 5 o'clock Friday morning. Her flight to New York was to leave at 2 a.m. the next day, which meant that she would have only twenty-one hours in the country—or nineteen hours not counting the time to and from the airport.

After a week of preparation for her visit, the two-day schedule of events had to be compressed into one.

The exhausted senator fell into bed for an hour or two, then rose for breakfast. After breakfast she was driven to a meeting with the president of the republic. Then the president gave a luncheon for her at the palace. After luncheon a car carried her to the museum of African art, traveling in a caravan of limousines with sirens in front to clear the street. The senator would have preferred to move about less conspicuously, so as perhaps to get a sense of people and their lives. She asked if the caravan could be disbanded, but that was impossible. Once the apparatus for receiving a foreign dignitary has been cranked into motion it is beyond anyone's power to stop.

At the museum door she was greeted by a considerable array of functionaries in dark suits and Senegalese costumes. A man in a blue robe had been designated as guide and explainer. He explained *everything*. In French, he explained a map on the wall for what seemed like an hour but probably was only about twenty minutes. He explained each object he came to in such excruciating detail that the eyes of the listeners glassed over, and time ran out before they could get to the second floor, where many of the finest objects are.

The senator had mentioned wanting to see a market and perhaps buy a few souvenirs and gifts. The caravan with sirens drove her not to a real market, where she might have met the man who walks naked or been approached by a fingerless leper or someone crawling without feet, or had some other unfortunate encounter, but rather to a government-sponsored craft market organized expressly for tourists.

There, two lines were waiting to greet her—one line of about forty men and another of twenty-five or so women. She was introduced to each one of these by name and shook their hands. Then she was led around the grounds, surrounded all the while by official people whose job it was to orchestrate her market visit. There was no opportunity to bargain with the merchants, which is the adventure of doing business here. If she expressed interest in something, someone in the retinue spoke privately to the merchant and bought it for her, and the seller was mute and powerless in the transaction. Probably sensing this unfair advantage, the senator expressed interest in few things, although there may have been some she really wanted.

As she was leaving, her hosts at the craft market made her a present of a large black wooden statue of the most garish and touristy genre, the bare torso of an African maiden with opulent polished breasts—the kind of monstrosity you might find in the recreation room of someone who keeps plastic flamingoes on the lawn outside. Her first thought had to be where in God's name she was going to hide the thing when she got it home.

Then the caravan bore her back to the Petit Palais, the government guest house, where the signature ahead of hers in the guest book was Yasser Arafat's. Sandwiches were sent up to her room. An hour later there was a press conference, and shortly after that she was delivered to a dinner in her honor at the residence of the American ambassador. Then she got to rest a little more before the sirens convoyed her back out to the airport.

As it happens, the senator is a very decent and intelligent woman who had come out to Africa in the genuine hope of learning some useful things. She deserved better.

The problem was partly structural—the inherent craziness of trying to visit seven countries in fourteen days. But the worse part was intentional—the unwillingness of other people to trust her to process and derive meaning from anything not carefully choreographed and sanitized in advance, and the heroic measures that therefore had been taken to prevent her from having what even remotely might be described as an African experience.

Essentially, then, she was at the mercy of what those other people, with their own agendas and their own axes to grind, saw fit to show or tell her. Traveling as a Very Important Person, if this is any example, is an arduous and arid affair. The wonder is that the people in a position to influence policy ever manage to learn anything at all.

43

LIKE A CANKER THAT WILL NOT HEAL, the denial of justice for the black majority in South Africa eats at the consciousness of Africans of every political persuasion. Always it is in their thoughts—tormenting them with frustration, anger and despair. For them, it is the issue above all others in the world, with no room for equivocation. Where one stands on the question defines absolutely, as far as they are concerned, one's moral credibility, one's position as friend or foe.

And invariably the subject does come up, as it has now in the office of the publisher of Senegal's national newspaper, *Le Soleil*.

Bara Diouf is a man of enormous vitality, grace and personal charm. He has that rare gift of elevating all around him to his own level of intensity. To watch him at work—especially to watch as he presides at the daily meeting of his newspaper's editorial board—is to understand that, as some men are destined to be yeomen, he was fated to be a leading player in whatever profession, in whatever country, chance might have placed him.

He is 60 years old, although he seems much younger. His education was at universities in Paris and Strasbourg in France.

He has traveled to nearly every part of the world, has been witness to Africa's decades of tumultuous evolution. He has relished influence, and has been humbled by nearly insupportable personal grief. And the result of all that is a human being of rare completeness. If this sounds a bit effusive, it can't be helped. He is a singular man.

But now, in late afternoon at his office on the newspaper's upper floor, with the last of the sun reflecting from the underside of gathering clouds and filling the room with a strange amber glow, he is talking about South Africa—about the hesitancy of the Europeans, and particularly of the Americans, to act decisively to break the tragic racist stalemate there. And gradually, as he speaks, a startling change comes over him.

"The values of the West," he has said, "are the values we have chosen. The concepts of liberty, of the rights of man, of human dignity, of justice—they are the ideas central to western civilization, on which the United States itself was founded. We have taken them for our own."

His voice, usually so gracious and composed, rises in pitch.

"But those are exactly the values that are being violated now in South Africa. And suddenly it seems they are not so sacred, after all. *Not there. Not for Africans.* Why? Why?"

His hands tremble. A lifetime of urbanity yields to the anguish of the suppurating wound.

"The president of this country . . . and Leopold Senghor before him . . . I, and men like myself—we have chosen. We are part of the West. It is irrevocable."

He is overcome now by fury. And though he and his visitor are colleagues and friends, when he raises his face his eyes burn with the resentment of a stranger's. It is no play-acting. He is a man afire to the very heart with rage.

"We have chosen," he says again. "And I tell you that sometimes I am *ashamed*. Write it!" The words are a vehement hiss. "Write that I am ashamed to find myself in your camp."

44

MISFORTUNE UPON MISFORTUNE and plague upon plague. One after another, the woes multiply.

Three good rains there have been in this single week. The first was a quick, hard shower; the second an early morning drenching; this latest a ten-hour inundation that began at midevening yesterday, dropped pea-sized hail for several minutes, then continued unabated until after daylight today.

Those storm fronts all swept from seaward across the peninsula and on toward the interior. Yet in a country that lives or perishes according to the rainfall, there was no leisure for rejoicing, no time to contemplate deliverance. Because disaster has come wearing a new face—a face with a billion mandibles clicking, clicking, devouring the hopes of another year.

Several weeks ago, when warnings began to circulate of an impending invasion of locusts and grasshoppers, the threat seemed incredible and remote. Now, of a sudden, the locusts are here—and not just here. There are reports of them multiplying and swarming over much of Africa in numbers unheard of since the 1930s.

In Senegal alone, the infestation spreads over some 400,000 hectares, nearly a million acres, in vital agricultural districts in the northern and north-central parts of the country. Twenty of the creatures to one square meter is said to be the density at which serious crop damage begins. From some areas of the north, concentrations of *two hundred* to the meter have been reported.

People who have seen a locust swarm rise up in a living cloud to darken the light of day, then sweep down upon the land to strip it bare as a desert, say that it is an amazing and awful thing to witness. One such swarm is able in a single day to consume 80,000 tons of cereal crops—enough to feed 50,000 people for a whole year. In a region where hunger already is a habit and the margins are fine, the result of such losses can be readily enough imagined. A Senegalese friend even ventured a prediction, the other day, that if the locusts could not be stopped, the government might fall—one of Africa's few democracies, smitten down by a bug.

Four giant propeller aircraft, contracted by an emergency grant from the American government, arrived this week at the airport north of the city to begin the counterattack. It is the first time large planes have been used for crop spraying in Africa. Each early morning, weather allowing, the planes take off with a roar, climbing over the fishing village of Yoff and banking out over the sea, headed up toward the Senegal River to lay another wide swath of pesticide. The big planes will be followed later by small aircraft and ground crews from other countries and international aid organizations.

But it is a massive undertaking, and time is no ally. Another generation of locusts has laid its eggs, and if those hatch and mature before the infestation is conquered, the number of insects will increase exponentially. The bug people say that would mean disastrous crop losses for at least the next three years.

187

First unrelieved years of drought. And now clouds of grasshoppers racing the farmers of the Sahel for the harvest. Like the fulfillment of some biblical curse, calamities as old as history itself grip Africa's millions in cycles of unending pain.

What happened in all the centuries before there were planes and chemical sprays and gifts of food from afar and other such means of surviving, of fighting back? *People died,* was what happened. Obscurely, by their inestimable millions, they died and went to dust. They could again.

45

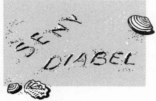

THE FUTURE SHINES MOST BRIGHTLY in the eyes of children, who do not yet know how hard the future is to grasp. And that undoubting hope is what makes them beautiful.

At Yoff village, where the American goes occasionally to fish, are two small boys who have appointed themselves his regular aides and friends. They are 10 or maybe 11 years old. One is the son of the mechanic who repairs the outboard motors of the local fishermen. The other lives with his mother, who is one of the women who sort and sell the catch the fishermen bring in. They are neither better off nor poorer than the other families of the village, which is to say that their lives, while endurable, are nevertheless hard and very spare.

Those two latched on to the American the first time he came there. Now, whenever he appears in his car at the top of the beach, they come running with a happy wave. One of them hurries to notify the boatman, Ouzin, that he has arrived. The other helps unload the car. Then, together, they carry his gear down the long slant of beach to the pirogue. During the several

Sény (left) and Diabel

hours he is out in the boat, they are the *gardiens* of the car. They are proud of that job and take it seriously; it pays them 50 cents each for the day.

You could never hope to see two more appealing youngsters anywhere. Their smiles are quick and open. There is about them a precocious sparkle, an air of intense and happy expectation, that sets them a bit apart.

The American asked one day what they would study when school began again in October. But they were finished with school, they told him. In their households, he guessed, the few dollars for books and transportation could not be spared. He was sick to hear it, and could not help wondering how long it would be until the light in those wonderfully animate faces went out.

He wanted to know their names, and they wrote them with their fingers in the sand of the beach. *Sény*, wrote one, and *Diabel* wrote the other. The motor repairman came over to the car to say hello. "Why don't you take my boy back with you to America?" he asked, and laughed at the extravagance of that notion.

"Sure," the American said. "Why not?"—because the truth was it already had crossed his mind, taking both of them back. The world does not have many like that to waste.

Not that there is anything *wrong* with the lives they will have. But, with just a chance, what might those two be? *Anything,* he thought. *They could be anything.* With some children you know right away there isn't any limit.

"Why not?" he said again. But the father, chuckling, taking it for a joke, was already turning away.

And in the few moments before the American went down to the boat, the wind off the ocean, stirring the flour-fine sand, had erased the names completely.

191

46

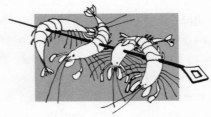

AT THE BASE OF THE VOLCANIC PLATEAU on which the city is perched, the ocean eternally comes beating in upon the rocks, grinding, carving, shaping this coast of Africa to its will. And down there near the tides, on a pier out-thrust over the water, is a restaurant upon whose physical setting it is hard to imagine that very many beaneries anywhere could improve.

Drink from the Nile, the Egyptians tell you, and you're sure to return some day to Cairo. That formula probably has sent more than a few romantics to the hospital with amoebas, bilharzia or worse.

But eat some evening at the Lagon I restaurant, with the waves breaking just below you and the skewered prawns grilled to pink perfection and the night sea breeze blowing the heat of the day away, and there will indeed be every likelihood of your coming back to Dakar.

Look one way from your table on the pier and you see the Isle of Gorée, riding the dark water like a ship, its outline revealed by only a few faint points of light. Straight out to seaward are real ships, freighters standing off almost at the horizon to await their turn in port, glowing as if in celebration of journey's end. On the other side, the shore bends away sharply under black cliffs toward a stony cape.

The air is fresh and sea-smelling. Any malarial mosquitoes are blown off on the wind. The lamps on the tables throw out circles of soft light that reflect under umbrellas and shine on the faces gathered there—African faces and European ones and both together—so that each table seems a distinct community, set apart in the congenial privacy of its own light.

The restaurant's owner, a Corsican, comes to the table of the Americans to ask if they are happy and if everything is all right. It's not just empty courtesy; he asks as if really wanting to know. So the American tells him that it was here at one of these tables, on a night almost exactly a year ago, that the notion first came to mind of living a summer in Africa, and that it had turned out to be a good idea. The Corsican seems immensely pleased by that. And a moment later the waiter brings a bottle of whiskey open to the table.

The pier gives ever-so-little shudders as the night swells come rolling under it to break and spout at the foot of the cliff, and then rush out again in trails of phosphorescent foam.

You can say that the Lagon is not Africa, any more than are the luxury hotels and villas and balconied townhouses that stand behind and above it, fronting the high coast road. They are foreign accretions, deposited and clinging like barnacles to this bend of azure shore. You can say that the *real* Africa is the more than eleven and one-half million square miles of desperation and painful striving that lies beyond that thin veneer of privilege. And that is true, of course.

But still it is an enchanted place, this restaurant on the pier out over the water. And there is a fair chance, if you ever stop there, that it will bring you back to see the rest.

47

ANOTHER DAY IS MOVING toward its end. Moussa, the old warrior, has come back from his annual leave and is sitting again on his metal chair at the edge of the garden, beside the gate. Like the prayer beads he passes through his fingers, the days have gone almost without notice—each with its own special meaning, yet all very much alike.

Dialo, the gardener, has started the sprinkler turning over the lawn and the flowers. The time for the rains is passing, maybe past, and this year, again, the rains were late. But you would never know it from the verdancy of the grounds. In Dialo's walled kingdom, plants never wither, no drought ever comes.

Dear Khadi, the house maid, has finished her work and gone to her quarters at the back of the garden, behind the kitchen. On each of the upstairs beds waits a fresh stack of things laundered and beautifully pressed. For the people of the house, it is a small miracle that is repeated each day, without effort. One wonders if her slender arm ever aches from the weight of the iron, and whether she must not sometimes despise the many clothes her people wear.

From Bocar's stove come the good smells of supper starting. The cake he baked earlier is cooling on the table. Now he is busy at the *crevettes beignets*—fresh shrimp washed and peeled, then dipped in a batter and put to sizzle and puff in the oil.

For a time several weeks ago, Bocar's bright spirit failed and worry overtook him. Every day he had headaches, and his vision blurred. It frightened him, less for himself than for his children. Suppose the problem were serious. Who would provide for the family of a cook gone blind? He went for an examination. The trouble, it turned out, was only that he needed glasses. He has them now, and they give his handsome face a studious look. The people of the house call him The Professor, and he laughs with them at that. The headaches are gone, his vision has perfectly cleared. The worry for his family has been dispelled, and he presides in his kitchen with a quick proud step, his face breaking suddenly into a smile that lights all around him.

That's how it is now—a little world in order. That's how one wishes it might remain. But one cannot help thinking of the fragility of all these lives.

The Americans will leave, and the regular family of the house will come back to live again. But even though it is measured in years, not weeks or months, their time here also will end. Duty will call them to some other place in another country. One day the movers will come to put everything in boxes and load the boxes on a truck to be taken to a ship.

There will be a moment for hurried goodbyes. Then those people, too, will be gone from here as certainly and as far as if they had vanished to another planet. A new life will unfold ahead of them. But not for the ones who are left behind, their whole hopes depending on the letters of recommendation that may or may not be enough to save them.

Who can know what the next people will be like?

They will know nothing of old Moussa's history or the hurt of his wounds. Or of Dialo's faithfulness to his plants. Or

Khadi's sweetness and how lovely she can be when, at special times, she dresses in her finest *boubou*. Or of Bocar's *crevettes*, or his care in keeping the refrigerator always filled with cold bottles of filtered water, or the luncheon salads he arranges prettily as flowers.

Maybe the new people will never know any of that. Maybe they will make different arrangements. Change has no memory. For the small people in a place like this, dependent always on accident and blind caprice, nothing ever is certain. Sickness spares or breaks them. Rains come or fail. The people they serve remain or go. The world tips, and with an awful casualness they are spilled off its edge.

Colonialism gave way to independence. New nations were born. Different leaders came to power, proclaiming new policies and new alignments. But for the small and the powerless, uncertainty and vulnerability remain the only constant truths. The meek do not inherit the Earth.

With Moussa by the gate

48

THE *CAP VERT* PENINSULA thrusts abruptly into the sea from the rounded bulge of West Africa, pointing toward the Americas. And this rocky spit, the Pointe des Almadies, is the outermost tip of the tip.

Follow the 15th parallel due west from here and after a journey of some 4,000 miles you make landfall in Central America at about the border between Honduras and Nicaragua. Or bear a few degrees north and you pass just above the West Indies to strike the coast of Florida. A few degrees more, and the destination becomes New York.

It somehow touches the imagination and the heart just to stand here and take one's bearings and consider.

To the left down the receding coast is the Dakar lighthouse, perched atop its precipitous hill, and just past that the start of Dakar city. To the right, although unseen around another jutting headland, are the fishing villages of N'Gor and Yoff, where life still is regulated by the strong, slow pull of the tides. Straight out ahead is the broken carcass of a ship and part of another, rusting on the reef that claimed them. And beyond that, nothing. Nothing except the sea, which, for most of the human experience, has divided the tribes of men one from the other, sharpened their differences and shaped their destinies.

Military strategists, believing that geography and perhaps all Nature ought to be organized around their plans for war, speak of this reach of ocean between West Africa and the Americas as the Atlantic Narrows. Which only goes to show that perspective is everything. Ships can cross those "narrows" in days, planes in hours, a spacecraft in thirty-three minutes. But for other, more valuable and more complicated things—prosperity, institutions of rational and humane government, concepts of human rights and dignity—the passage has proved to be much longer. The question, increasingly, is whether it ever can be made at all.

Roughly a quarter of a century has elapsed, now, since this country and most of the others in Africa achieved their independence. The bright hopes of those early years have been blown away like smoke. Gone, with them, is much of the idealism. The mood of Africans today, taken as a whole, is of bafflement and gnawing despair. It can be said that twenty-five or thirty years are only a moment in history, and that other societies have taken far longer to pass from early turbulence to the fullness of their maturity. But the unhappy and perhaps unfair truth is that precisely what Africa does not have is the luxury of time.

There's no doubt that luck has been against this continent— evil weather, an unfavorable world economy and all the rest. But more than just luck has been at work. In many cases the corrupt few have become richer, whereas, for the rest, "freedom" has been translated into even crueler oppression, even more degrading poverty. Refugees from famine, war and the brutality of their rulers are adrift by the millions across Africa. Cultivable land retreats as the desert advances. In the fallacious belief that survival may rest in numbers, Africans are reproducing at a rate that will double the continent's population sometime early in the next century.

What has passed for leadership in certain of the African states has been venal, abusive, inept and in some cases downright farcical—a monstrous stage show of blood, polemics and elaborate ceremony, having nothing at all to do with those humble questions of life and death that affect the poor and the disillusioned who are the governed.

As a friend with long experience in Africa said the other day, "There is no tragedy in farce. The tragedy is in a country like Senegal, which is doing a lot of things right—and which still might not make it."

In the face of very great hardship, one finds here a surprising degree of tolerance, of civility, even of imperfect democracy (as all democracies, by their very nature, are imperfect). There is a good deal of pluralism and free expression. The processes of law generally are respected. The country is led—to the extent it can be led—by a president who is not only an honest and able man but also a realist. Not the least of his gifts, because he knows that survival depends on it, has been his ability to make his country's case for substantial aid from the rich donors of the West.

Yet for all this, so many and great are the problems, and so slender the resources, that by most objective measures—economic performance, per capita income, food production, the ability to provide essential services—Senegal, too, is slipping backward. Not as dramatically or as violently as one sees elsewhere, but slipping, slipping, all the same.

Opportunity is a word that has all but disappeared from the vocabulary of the young, except for a tiny minority of the well-born or well-connected. What happens when people lose faith in education and diligence as keys to the door of a reasonable future? Is that not a fuse which, once lighted, burns to an ominous end? And is there not some point at which even those nations that wish Africa well might be tempted to look away, in fatigue and futility, from further involvement in an ordeal that appears to have no end?

"Where has it gone wrong?" a Senegalese, a man of influence in his country's affairs, was heard to remark in a tone of introspection and pain. "We're in a hole from which no reasonable mind, my own included, can see how we will extricate ourselves. I wake in the night, sometimes, wishing that I still lived in a French colony."

A quarter-century after independence, sadder words than his hardly can be imagined. How long does it go on? Where does it finally end? Those are the questions that turn in the mind as one stands, listening to the waves lap, contemplating the unbridged distances between men, and looking out from this stony point at Africa's edge.

Pointe des Almadies